Reengineering Your Nonprofit Organization:
A Guide to Strategic Transformation

NONPROFIT, LAW, FINANCE, AND MANAGEMENT SERIES

Reengineering Your Nonprofit Organization: A Guide to Strategic Transformation

Alceste T. Pappas, Ph.D.
Pappas Consulting Group Inc.

John Wiley & Sons, Inc.

New York • Chichester • Brisbane • Toronto • Singapore

Copyright © 1996 by John Wiley & Sons, Inc.

Library of Congress Cataloging in Publication Data:
Pappas, Alceste T.
    Reengineering your nonprofit organization : a guide to strategic
    transformation / Alceste T. Pappas.
        p.   cm.— (Nonprofit law, finance and management series)
    Includes bibliographical references.
    ISBN 0-471-11807-9 (cloth : alk. paper)
    1. Nonprofit organizations—Management.   2. Reengineering
(Management)   3. Strategic planning.   I. Title.   II. Series.
HD62.6.037   1995
658.4'063—dc20   95-400
                                                                        CIP

Printed in the United States of America

10 9 8 7 6 5 4 3 2 1

Dedication

To my late grandmother, Andromache Hero, and my mother, Thetis Hero Pappas, who instilled in me a passion for the world of the nonprofit. Especially to my mother who always brought me with her as she worked with my grandmother in founding the Philoptochos of St. Paul's Greek Orthodox Church of Long Island, New York.

To my deceased mother-in-law, Minka Endich, who lived her life in constant charity and who was active in a myriad of Jewish women's organizations.

To all of those special men in my life who constantly and lovingly encouraged me to become and remain a professional with heart:

—my husband, Sylvan V. Endich, my best friend and supporter, who served as my research assistant throughout this endeavor

—my late father, Costas E. (Gus) Pappas, who always believed in me no matter what my eccentricities

—my father-in-law, Jerome Endich, who is the living exemplification of a rabbi

—my brother, Dr. Conrad T. E. Pappas, a neurosurgeon with compassion and tenacity

—Robert F. Kerley, Charles A. Nelson, Daniel D. Robinson, and Frederick J. Turk, who were each destined to be bosses and mentors and who, most ironically, had known each other before I knew them.

Contents

Preface

The world of the nonprofit comprises many different lines or "sectors or industries," each with its own mission and constituency. Among these are hospitals, social services organizations, schools, colleges, universities, churches and other forms of organized religion, cultural organizations such as museums and performing arts organizations, international relief organizations, foundations, trade associations, and so on.

Although the fundamental tenets that are expounded in the management texts for the for-profit or corporate sector are typically applicable to the nonprofit, some fundamental attributes and operating principles distinguish the sectors. The most fundamental is the mission-based rather than bottom-line focus of the nonprofit. Although the nonprofit must generate sufficient resources to cover its operating costs and create reserves for its future, it does not exist to make a profit. Rather, it exists to do good works and enable society to be a better place than it would be if its entire focus were monetary. Additionally, the nonprofit looks not only to a paid staff of dedicated workers but to an unpaid staff as well. These unpaid staff or volunteers serve their organizations on a day-to-day basis and in the board room. Finally, the nonprofit is driven by its constituents, those who contribute to it, those who work for it, as well as those who avail themselves of the programs and services it provides.

The world of reengineering has its roots in the corporate sector. Although *reengineering* is perceived among some as the "hottest management buzzword of the '90s" (Hal Lancaster, "Managing Your Career," *Wall Street Journal*, January 17, 1995, p. B1), reengineering has its roots in decades of thoughtful work that has focused on systems theory and on continuous quality improvement.

Indeed, it was Hammer and Champy's 1993 text, *Re-Engineering the Corporation* (New York: Harper Business), that popularized and brought to another level what many corporate types had been attempting—to make their businesses more profitable and restore the confidence of shareholders. Hammer and Champy describe reengineering as *the fundamental rethinking and redesign of business processes to achieve dramatic improvements in performance such as cost, quality, service, and speed.*

Since the publication of their book and their onslaught on the public speaking circuit, many popular texts have provided corporate case examples of success, and, most recently, a growing numbers of articles and texts have refuted the panacea attributed to reengineering. In fact, some are attributing the almost uncontrollable wave of corporate reengineering to the creation of employee and management stress and corporate anorexia.

The bottom line is that *reengineering equals radical change*. As Dr. Donna Stoddard eerily described in her lecture at the Twenty-First Century Higher Education Conference sponsored by KPMG Peat Marwick in December of 1994, "Reengineering is like changing the engines of a flying airplane." Having made that statement, what place does reengineering have in the nonprofit world? That question is the right one to ask. In the minds of many, the nonprofit world is characterized by stability if not tranquillity. It is viewed as special or somehow beyond the fray; "it does God's work" and is above scrutiny, let alone self-assessment. Others believe that it represents a public trust and demands ongoing scrutiny and accountability. This cry for accountability results in large measure from the sacredness, if you will, of donated dollars and the need for donors to know that their hard-earned dollars have been applied to program and service delivery rather than to administrative overhead.

The truth of the matter is that nonprofit organizations, no matter how large or small, are subject to the vicissitudes of funding, financial support, market position, and strength of leadership, just as their for-profit counterparts. As such, they are vulnerable and not guaranteed "God's good graces" just because they do good works.

This vulnerability, combined with the overwhelming revolution of change throughout the world and the unique role of the nonprofit in the history of the United States, demands a text such as this geared specifically to the unique character, legacy, and role of the nonprofit.

Will reengineering disappear from the annals of management texts or the lips of managers? We doubt that it will. Although the use of reengineering as a buzzword may indeed disappear or be replaced by yet another word or phrase, the inherent need to engage in continuous self-assessment will remain through our lifetime. Indeed, we would argue that cyberspace, which is rapidly replacing our ancestors' bucolic view of life and work, will only escalate the pace of such change.

Historically, the nonprofit sector has taken its lead for change from the corporate sector. The world of health care within the nonprofit marketplace has been in the throes of fundamental change for at least the past decade and is currently confounded with an entire restructuring of its delivery and financing mechanisms. Arts and cultural institutions, trade associations, foundations, colleges, universities, schools, churches, and other such groups have only recently concluded that tweaking around the edges or across-the-board cuts are not sufficient to ensure an organization's ability to continue to fulfill its fundamental mission.

In short, most nonprofits are in pain. Their senior staff and their board members feel the pain acutely in their attempts to balance budgets and raise funds for their good causes. Pain is a magnificent motivator. It is in this context that many organizations are asking themselves fundamental questions about the very reason for their being.

As nonprofits are the essence of the American "commitment to responsible citizenship in the community" (Peter Drucker in his preface to his 1990 book, *Managing the Nonprofit Organization*, published by HarperCollins), we must find ways to ensure that they are well positioned in this complex and stressed time of ours. Clearly, one of the most profound ways in which this sector can ensure its long-term survival is through thoughtful and honest scrutiny at all levels within the organization—from the board level through the most junior staff members as well as the volunteers.

Indeed, all must play a role in ensuring that their organization's founding mission is serving its constituency in the most effective and efficient manner possible. Reengineering, if properly applied, can afford these volunteers and the staff an opportunity for new life and recommitment to institutional mission while ensuring that its programs and services are delivered in the least costly manner possible.

We trust that this book will afford practitioners, volunteers, and the student of the nonprofit an understanding of how reengineering can assist in the transformation of their organization. Case examples are cited throughout to provide an understanding of what some staff and volunteers are finding out about their own organizations as they begin the task of clean-slate assessment.

Each of the nine chapters in this book is geared to provide a theoretical framework followed by practical, hands-on experience within the sector. Lessons to be learned are summarized at the conclusion of each chapter.

We first provide an overview of the nonprofit sector. We know we are talking to the converted, but we want to give you some compelling data about the nonprofit that you could share with those you want to involve in your organization. We then address the precursors to reengineering—strategic planning and resource allocation. In the next chapter, we present a definition of reengineering that takes into account the idiosyncrasies of the nonprofit. Discussions in the next four chapters concerning the role of the volunteer on a day-to-day level as well as at the board level address the profound need to redesign the expectations and responsibilities of the volunteer.

The remaining chapters also address ways in which to manage human resources from both the volunteer and paid staff perspective in a new and exciting way to reenforce the mission of the reengineered nonprofit, and we present some thought-provoking ways to reengineer relationships with other entities—be they for-profit, nonprofit, or governmental.

In the next to last chapter, we attempt to define a conceptual framework for performance measurement and accountability. This text concludes with a chapter dedicated to the fundamental redefinition or transformation that can proceed from reengineering if there is the will to do so.

We sincerely hope that this book provides those involved in delivering critical programs and services in the nonprofit sector with an understanding of what it takes to manage an organization in an age of technological revolution and societal turmoil. The nonprofit cannot fail. This world of ours needs the programs and services of the nonprofit more than ever before, and the world desperately needs them to do an even more compelling and better job at what they are doing.

Alceste T. Pappas, Ph.D.
July 1995

Acknowledgments

In so many ways, this book has been an extended family effort. First and foremost, I must thank my husband, Sylvan V. Endich, for his hours of research and analysis. Without his tireless patience, this book would still be a dream. In addition, I am forever grateful for the outstanding group of young women who serve as my support and extended family in the workplace. My thanks to Barbara Carlucci, the chief operating officer of the Pappas Consulting Group, as well as to Christine Schwartz, Cathy Casey, and Eileen Gleeson. Without them individually or collectively, I would never have been able to focus my energies and schedule to conclude this endeavor. Special thanks as well to Christine, Cathy, and Eileen for their research, word-processing, and graphics efforts.

And, finally, thank you to so many friends and clients in the nonprofit world who have taught me what a special yet vexing environment it is. You have emboldened me to share not only what I have learned from you but also what I hope I have given to you in some small measure.

CHAPTER ONE

Setting the Context for Transformation

ANATOMY OF THE NONPROFIT SECTOR

From a clinical perspective, a *nonprofit organization* is any private organization that provides services of benefit to society without financial incentive and that qualifies as a section 501 (c) (3) organization under the Internal Revenue code. From a passionate perspective, nonprofits engage in activities and enlist the support of millions of men, women, and children to provide a mechanism for self-help; for voluntary assistance to those in physical, financial, or psychic need; and for the pursuit of a wide array of beliefs and interests.

There are six defining characteristics of the nonprofit sector:

1. *Formally constituted/institutionalized.* Nonprofit organizations have bylaws and are legally constituted entities with their own IRS classification.

2. *Private, as opposed to governmental.* The federal government and state and municipal entities have a different IRS classification and are considered in the public domain. Nonprofits, on the other hand, are often considered to be a third sector after government and the corporate world.

3. *Not profit distributing.* If a nonprofit organization generates an excess of revenues over expenditures (profit) in any given year, the profits must be plowed back into the organization to support its fundamental mission. The profits cannot be distributed to the organization's founders, managers, leaders, volunteers, or staff.

4. *Self-governing.* Each nonprofit has a board of directors or trustees that holds the organization's assets in public trust. To this end, the directors/trustees have fiduciary and legal responsibility for the

entity. There are codes of conduct that call for board members to refrain from conflicts of interest and personal self-aggrandizement.

5. *Voluntary.* Perhaps one of the most distinguishing characteristics of this sector is its dependence on the goodwill and countless hours of contributed services provided by volunteers. The giving of one's time for the greater good is an extraordinary asset that allows the nonprofit sector to provide services and programs at less than their true or total cost.

6. *Of public benefit.* The nonprofit sector encourages individual initiative for the public good, just as businesses and corporations encourage individual and collective action for the private good or profit motive.

The nonprofit sector is basically clustered into five groups:

1. *Health care*, including hospitals, clinics, nursing and personal care facilities, home health care centers, and specialty facilities.

2. *Education*, including elementary and secondary education, higher education, libraries, vocational schools, noncommercial research institutes, and related educational services.

3. *Social and legal Services*, including individual and family social services, housing, job training and vocational rehabilitation services, residential care, day care, and legal aid services.

4. *Civic and Social*, including advocacy organizations, civil rights organizations, and neighborhood-based organizations.

5. *Arts and culture*, including orchestras, theater groups, museums, art galleries, and botanical and zoological gardens.

The commissioner of Internal Revenue reports that there were 1,140,000 nonprofit entities in the United States in 1989 (see Exhibit 1–1).

When we begin to investigate further, the makeup of the nonprofit entities reported by the IRS, some interesting data emerge that reflect the relative size and expenditures of the five clusterings of nonprofit organizations, as well as the extraordinary diversity in shape and size of this sector (see Exhibit 1–2).

As of 1989, the latest date for which data are available from the U.S. Census Bureau, there were approximately 360,000 active nonprofit, public service organizations. Of these, even more precise data are available for the 164,360 organizations that have at least one paid employee:

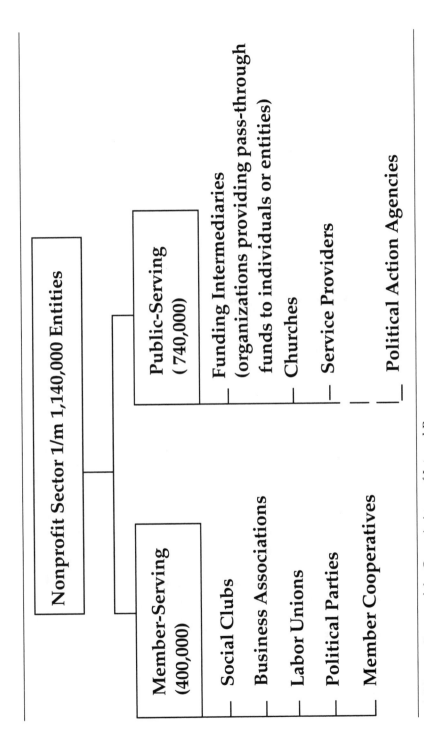

Nonprofit Sector 1/m 1,140,000 Entities

Member-Serving (400,000)

- Social Clubs
- Business Associations
- Labor Unions
- Political Parties
- Member Cooperatives

Public-Serving (740,000)

- Funding Intermediaries (organizations providing pass-through funds to individuals or entities)
- Churches
- Service Providers
- Political Action Agencies

Exhibit 1–1 Report of the Commissioner of Internal Revenue
Source: Washington: U.S. Government Printing Office, 1989.

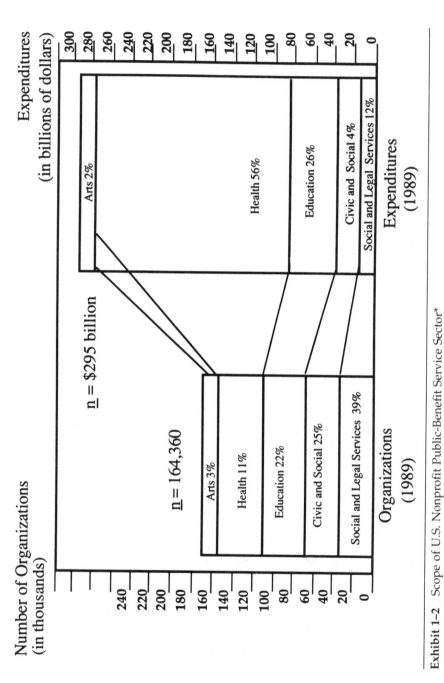

Number of Organizations (in thousands)

Expenditures (in billions of dollars)

n = $295 billion

n = 164,360

Arts 3%

Health 11%

Education 22%

Civic and Social 25%

Social and Legal Services 39%

Arts 2%

Health 56%

Education 26%

Civic and Social 4%

Social and Legal Services 12%

Organizations (1989)

Expenditures (1989)

Exhibit 1–2 Scope of U.S. Nonprofit Public-Benefit Service Sector*

Source: U.S. Census Bureau [1991]; U.S. Department of Education [1991]; Hodgkinson and Weitzman [1992].

4

- The *social services agencies* are the most numerous. Close to 40% of all nonprofit organizations fall into this category, yet these entities account for only 12% of total expenditures, underscoring the large number of such agencies and the tremendous competition for resources in this arena.

- The next largest group are the *civic and social organizations*, which include neighborhood associations, advocacy organizations, civil rights organizations, and so on. Twenty-five percent of nonprofit organizations assume this form yet account for only 4% of total expenditures, revealing the myriad of small entities in this cluster.

- Another 22% of the nonprofit organizations are *educational institutions*, including private elementary and secondary schools as well as private universities and colleges.

- *Health organizations*, including hospitals, nursing homes, and clinics, comprise 11% of all such organizations yet account for over half or 56% of the total expenditures reported. These figures simply underscore the magnitude of the financial impact of this particular market on the U.S. economy and the high stakes in the health care reform movement.

- The smallest component of the nonprofit service sector is the *arts and culture* component, which includes symphonies, art galleries, theaters, zoos, and other cultural institutions. Together these represent 3% of the nonprofit organizations.

THE NONPROFIT SECTOR AS AN ECONOMIC FORCE

The nonprofit sector has expenditures as well as revenues, just like the corporate sector. However, what most Americans do not truly understand is that the nonprofit sector is a considerable force in the American economy. In 1989, for example, this sector had operating expenses in excess of $295 billion, the equivalent of 6% of the U.S. gross national product (computed from estimates developed in Hodgkinson, Weitzman et al. [1992]).

In addition, in that same year, federal, state, and local governments in the United States spent close to $956 billion—19% of the U.S. gross national product and more than half of all government spending on social, health, and educational programs (see Exhibit 1–3).

Hodgkinson et al. estimate that U.S. nonprofit public service organizations had revenues of approximately $343 billion in 1989. The major sources of income for the nonprofit are as follows (see Exhibits 1–4 and 1–5):

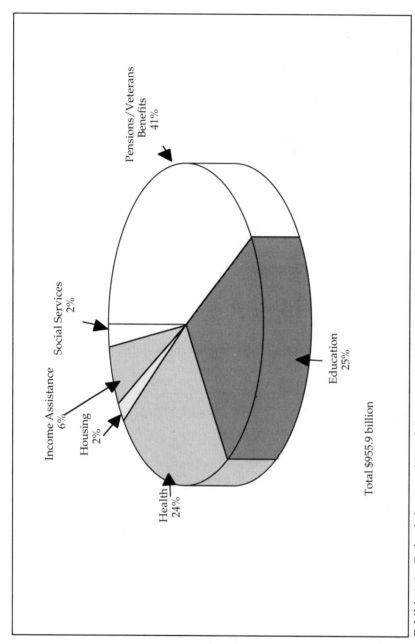

Exhibit 1-3 Federal, State, and Local Government Funding: Health, Education and Social Programs, 1989

Source: Compiled from data in Bixby [November, 1991].

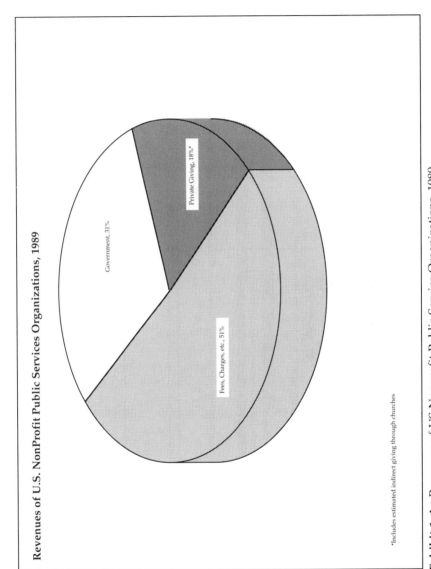

Revenues of U.S. NonProfit Public Services Organizations, 1989

Government, 31%

Private Giving, 18%*

Fees, Charges, etc., 51%

*Includes estimated indirect giving through churches

Exhibit 1–4 Revenues of US Nonprofit Public Service Organizations, 1989

Source: Compiled from data in Hodgkinson and Weitzman [1992].

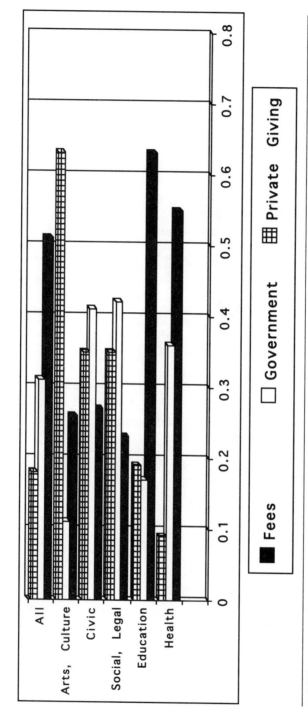

Exhibit 1–5 Nonprofit Organization Revenue by Type of Agency, 1989
Source: Compiled from data in Hodgkinson and Weitzman [1992].

- *Fees, service charges, and other commercial income,* including charges for hospital care not covered by government health insurance, other direct payment for services, income from sales of products, and college tuition payments. These sources alone account for more than half of all nonprofit service organization revenues.

- *Government,* the second largest source of income. Grants, contracts, and reimbursements reflect partnerships and alliances between government and the nonprofit sector in carrying out public purposes from the delivery of health care to the provision of education.

- *Private giving,* providing 18% of total income that nonprofits receive. It is the third largest source of nonprofit service organization income.

In addition to the income nonprofit service organizations receive, they are served by volunteers. Hodgkinson and Weitzman estimate that 98 million Americans volunteered an average of four hours a week to various charitable and other organizations in 1989. Public service nonprofit organizations are the beneficiaries of a significant portion of this largesse. Indeed, this volunteer labor translates to approximately 3 million full-time employees.

Can there be any question that the nonprofit sector is a formidable economic factor?

THE MISSION-BASED, CONSTITUENCY-DRIVEN NATURE OF THE NONPROFIT SECTOR

In essence, the United States is a three-sector society (the following is adapted from the *Resource Development System* © developed by KPMG Peat Marwick LLP):

1. *The private or corporate sector* developed in the late 1880s with the rise of industrialists. The sector was formulated to generate profits and working capital in order to grow the economy and, subsequently, the nation. Currently, it is undergoing significant self-assessment with the overriding drive of becoming more profitable than ever.

2. *The public or government sector* influence started to grow exponentially during the New Deal and the World War II era. It was government's fervent belief that it had a civic responsibility to provide for and protect each citizen. In the early 1990s, and in most dramatic fashion in the November 1994 elections, Americans perceived governmental agencies as purveyors of expensive and ineffective programs and services peopled with self-aggrandizing bureaucrats. Cries for slashing governmental waste have reached a crescendo.

3. *The nonprofit or third sector* has provided enterprising Americans the opportunity to take an idea or support a cause or provide a service in a manner that did not benefit them financially but rather bettered society as a whole or an element of it (for example, children, the elderly, AIDS research, or the eradication of polio). As with its private and public sector counterparts, the nonprofit sector is now confronted with a panoply of financial and other challenges that demand a fundamental rethinking of the way of providing education or health care or delivering much needed services for homeless people.

The nonprofit sector is driven by its mission, *not the bottom line.* It is driven by its various stakeholders or constituencies—those individuals who provide resources (time, money, physical assets) and who, in turn, expect a service, a "thank you," or a contractual relationship of some sort (e.g., a paycheck, a degree).

Decades ago, growing numbers of Americans became disenchanted with public-run services and identified community needs that were not being provided through either the private or the public sector. These needs included such services as counseling, training, shelter, and food and led to the birth of the nonprofit sector in the United States.

It is interesting that the lines that have historically divided the three sectors have been blurring, almost imperceptibly for the last three to four decades. For example, elements of the corporate, public, and nonprofit sectors are to be found in the development of the Tennessee Valley Authority, state government programs operated by the Salvation Army, municipal hospitals sold to for-profit hospital corporations, and so on.

Indeed, economic conditions are not only providing opportunities for such alliances and partnerships (see Chapter 5), they are also drawing the proverbial lines in the sand. For example, politicians eager to balance federal, state, and municipal budgets are hacking away at so-called entitlement programs such as welfare and looking to the nonprofit to expand its service levels. The debate over federal funding for the nation's public broadcasting system is just one such example.

CASE STUDY

The Battle over Federal Funding of the Nation's Public Broadcasting System

Currently, the federal government provides the Corporation for Public Broadcasting $300 million annually to distribute to public radio and television stations across the country.

Newt Gingrich, the speaker of the House of Representatives has proposed abolishing all such federal support. This federal money represents 16% of the revenues for public broadcasting. In 1993, public stations raised more than $943 million in private contributions.

During an interview on C-SPAN in January 1995, Mr. Gingrich said: "If you got a good product, people will donate. If you don't have a good product, why are you forcing working taxpayers to subsidize your plaything?"

In an interview quoted in the January 12, 1995, edition of the *Chronicle of Philanthropy*, Stanley S. Litow, director of corporate-support programs at the International Business Machines Corporation, said: "Private sector resources are already pretty well stretched."

In the same article, public broadcasting advocates reported: "Loss of federal aid could mean that many stations, especially small ones in rural areas, could be forced to close."

THE GUT-WRENCHING NINETIES AND THE LOOMING MILLENNIUM

The public broadcasting case study can be replicated across the entire nonprofit sector and its five major markets or clusters. It is obvious that this sector is under siege from an endless variety of constituencies. The sector can no longer bask in its historic glory and assume a business-as-usual approach. It is time that the sector becomes deliberate about how it manages itself. More than ever before, nonprofits will have to *intentionally*

- Focus on utilizing the resources of staff, volunteers, board members, and donors in a more integrated and productive manner.
- Assess the portfolio of programs and services offered from a zero-base (i.e., assume that the organization is being created from scratch and is being put together for the very first time) or clean-slate perspective to ensure that they support the organization's mission in the most effective (quality-service levels) and efficient (least costly) manner possible.
- Position themselves in a highly competitive marketplace through the generation and use of market research data.
- Diversify their revenue stream as financial resources shrink and competition for diminishing resources grows. Additionally, non-

profits will have to analyze carefully the sources of those revenues; ask what motivates individuals, foundations, and corporations to give; and ask the soul-searching question of what the organization provided in return to its constituents.

- Examine how the entity's assets (financial, physical, and human) are being managed and leveraged to ensure longevity.
- Balance the needs of individuals and their unique agendas with those of the organization as a whole.
- Exist as an integrated rather than an isolated set of functions, programs, activities, and services.

If the nonprofit is worthy of such transformation, what attributes must it retain to be worthy of survival? First and foremost, the sector must continue to focus on its mission and those served and hold those trusts inviolate. Second, the very special nature of the volunteer-staff partnership must be enhanced and celebrated. Third, board and senior leadership must exercise a firm commitment to a higher order of ethical standards. Fourth, employees must not be solely motivated by their paycheck but rather compelled by the mission and the duty to serve. Fifth, long-term outcomes must remain more important than instant results.

As the twenty-first century approaches, the values of care, service, and selflessness that the nonprofit sector inculcates must be preserved. These values, however, must be embedded in the context of constant change and self-examination. Now more than ever, the nonprofit sector needs millions of paid professional and support staff trained in nonprofit management or willing to eschew the for-profit workplace for the nonprofit world. Our next century desperately needs people to make a conscious decision to do good works, to impart values and knowledge, to make a new discovery, or to help those in need. We simply need the nonprofit sector to make society function with a set of values and belief systems that transcends the bottom line and the chase for ever-increasing profit margins.

CHAPTER TWO

Setting the Stage to Reengineer

Reengineering involves the fundamental redesign of a nonprofit's organizational structure, processes, service delivery mechanism, and technology. In our experience, such basic self-analysis cannot be done in a vacuum nor, can it be expected to yield sustained improvement in efficiency and service levels without an organization-wide or long term perspective. Indeed, if reengineering in the nonprofit sector is to be successful, senior staff and directors alike must first agree on a blueprint for the future. This blueprint cannot be created in the collective heads of the executive director and the board chair. Rather, the blueprint must emerge from a deliberate and deliberative strategic planning process. In turn, this strategic planning process must include a series of intentional and integrated resource allocation steps that stipulate operating and capital expenditures on an action step–by–action step basis.

MANAGERS AND DIRECTORS AS STRATEGIC DECISION MAKERS

When times were good and the coffers of the nonprofit were full if not overflowing, managers and directors expanded the number of programs and services to meet the budget. As the coffers began to diminish and nonprofits witnessed increasing financial constraints, those responsible for the well-being of their institutions had to become more adaptive and expert in predicting and avoiding problems. In the past several decades, as multiple external and internal forces have confronted the sector, managers and directors alike have begun to embrace the tenets of strategic planning in the corporate literature and have adapted them to their own particular nonprofit marketplace.

Consequently, executive directors of nonprofit entities have become responsible (as are their for-profit counterparts) for the following array of functions:

- Planning
- Organizing
- Staffing
- Directing
- Coordinating
- Reporting
- Budgeting

Good managers have come to learn through on-the-job training, mentorship, and/or professional development that they must weave their managerial magic and strategies through a maze of management practices, support structures, and human resources that is embedded in an organizational culture unique to their particular operating environment. In turn, each key business activity, service, or program is shaped by four elements: management practice, organizational culture, human resources, and support structures (see Exhibit 2–1).

INTERRELATIONSHIPS

One of the most daunting tasks for managers, volunteers, and staff is grasping the notion that nonprofit organizations are and behave like complex systems. *Systems theory* provides powerful insight into understanding the interrelationships that exist among and between people within an organization. Systems theory also provides insight into the multiple interrelationships one organization has with others within society as a whole.

1. A *system* is a set of two or more elements in which
   - The behavior of each element affects the behavior of the whole.
   - The behavior of the elements and their effects on the whole are interdependent.
2. A *purposeful system* is a system that exists to achieve specified ends (not just a random aggregation of elements).
3. An *organization* is a purposeful system that is
   - Part of one or more other purposeful systems.
   - Made up of parts (e.g., people) that have purposes of their own.

Management Practice	Organizational Culture	Human Resources	Support Structures
• Tactical Planning Process	• Beliefs	• Human Resource Planning	• Organization
• Management Reporting Systems	• Values	• Recruiting	• Communications Network
• Incentive Programs	• Expectations	• Training	
	• Style	• Integrating	
	• Norms		
	• Language		

Exhibit 2–1   Key Activities of the Nonprofit Operating Environment

15

For example, the YWCA of the USA has hundreds of community and student associations across the United States. In addition, the YWCA of the USA is part of the World YWCA. Therefore, what transpires at the World YWCA level will necessarily impact, either directly or indirectly, the national office of the YWCA of the USA and its board, as well as its hundreds of community and student associations. If the World YWCA decides that the "women's" component of its mission and name is no longer applicable, the repercussions will be felt in the national office as well as in the YWCA of Pittsburgh. This change would mean that the organization embraces men as well as women in its membership. This, in turn, has a profound impact on the kinds of programs and services offered in Pittsburgh, advocated at the national level, and espoused at the world level.

ORGANIZATIONAL CULTURE

The first step in preparing for the development of a strategic planning process and the plan itself is an understanding of the organization's *culture*—its beliefs, values, expectations, language, motivation, and norms. This understanding will enable staff and volunteers alike to develop a realistic set of expectations for the planning process as well as a realistic framework concerning how radical the plan can be. Organizational culture is often defined as "the way we do things here." It comprises the beliefs and values that typify the way in which the organization functions as well as the expectations people have of it.

Nonprofit organizational culture results from, is reinforced by, and/or is modified by five major factors: the organization's history; its structure and reporting relationships; its management practices or ways of doing business on a day-to-day basis; the manner in which it supports communication between and among its volunteers, staff, and board; and its reward systems, be they performance appraisal systems of individual incumbents or incentives for managing fiscal resources prudently (see Exhibit 2–2).

This initial culture assessment should be directed by the executive director prior to the strategic planning process. It should be structured in such a way as to include volunteers and staff throughout the organization in small-group discussions. Written survey instruments are frequently used to get employee and volunteer perceptions of the group's culture. As Exhibit 2–3 indicates, such a thoughtful process will help you to determine what your organization's culture will enable you to accomplish and what barriers will impede the implementation of certain programs and initiatives. In many ways, your organization's culture serves

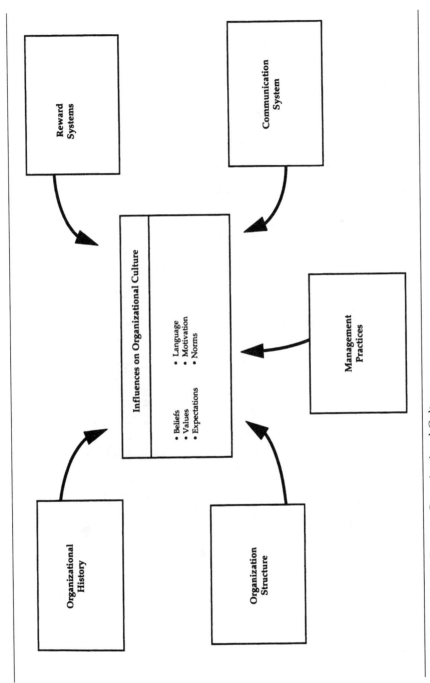

Exhibit 2–2   What Influences Organizational Culture

The Culture Screen

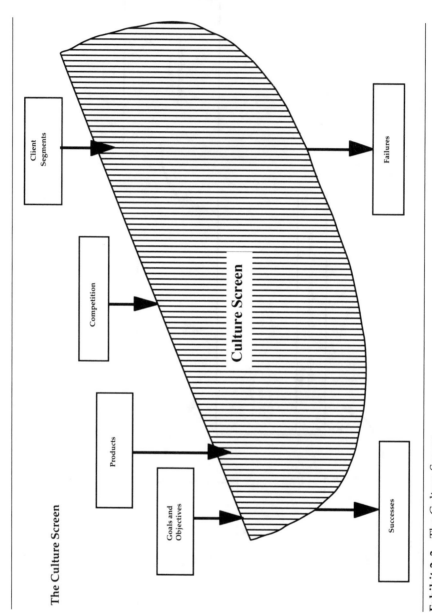

Exhibit 2-3   The Culture Screen

as a screen for determining what goals, objectives, and programs and services (products) will filter through the screen. In many ways, this culture assessment provides a reality check so that you can proceed with determining the logistics and organization of the planning process (also known as the *plan-to-plan*).

GETTING STARTED: THE PLAN-TO-PLAN

Upon completion of the cultural assessment, the executive director and the board chair must work in partnership to define the players and their roles in the planning process (see Exhibit 2–4).

The president/executive director, by virtue of her/his position, must serve as the nonprofit's locus for planning. Realistically, however, planning requires the appointment of a senior staff member to serve as the planning officer. The incumbent should possess technical and analytical skills and should have the trust of the organization. The person should have a thorough grasp of the role of technology in producing and maintaining an organization-wide database that would contain data elements critical to strategic decision making (for example, the demography of the region, socioeconomic status of users/clients, economic trends in the region, staff turnover within the organization, financial trend lines for the organization and so on.). This planning officer should have a basic grasp of institutional research (both internal as well as external data) and

The players	Their role
• Governing Board	—Organizes itself to oversee planning and approve major recommendations
• President/Executive Director	—Is the chief planning officer
• Planning Officer (or Staff)	—Serves as technical advisor to and guardian of the strategic planning process —Organizes data, prepares documents, and plans meetings
• Senior Managers	—Constitute the planning team or planning leadership
• Managers, Faculty, Staff, Students, Alumni, State Agencies, Volunteers, Other Stakeholders	—Participate appropriately, as defined by the process

Exhibit 2–4 The Players and Their Roles

either be directly responsible for or be part of the team that asks those responsible to provide preliminary budget information, summarizes such data, and creates an organization-wide budget document.

As planning officer, this person should ultimately assume responsibility for coordinating the organization's reengineering process and conducting work sessions. The incumbent not only collects, interprets, and disseminates the data for the planning and budgeting process, but also prepares electronic spreadsheets and other formats for participants to use in the process. This approach and the role of the planning officer ensures the consistency of response from all levels of the organization and its board and brings discipline and credibility to the process.

During such working sessions, the first requirement is to stipulate the players and their respective roles, as well as the degree to which the parties will get involved in actual decision making as opposed to providing insight/input, serving in an advisory capacity, and so on. Additionally, it will be critical, especially for multidimensional entities (e.g., state system of higher learning or a national social service agency with multiple chapters) to determine what existing governance mechanisms should be consulted (e.g., faculty senates or local boards) throughout the process so that every part of the entity has a sense of involvement in the process.

Second, it is critical to define the strategic planning process. For example, the specific steps that will be undertaken to complete the development of the strategic plan should be stipulated, as well as the period of time the plan itself will cover. The six-phase strategic planning outline in Exhibit 2–5 provides the skeleton on which your organization can define, in its own terms, what constitutes each specific step or task.

The timeline for any strategic planning process must be constructed on several levels. First, determine the period of time the plan will address. Most nonprofit organizations choose a three-to-five–year time frame, with many opting for three years because the speed with which such conditions as interest rates and the Consumer Price Index change and impact the organization can accelerate exponentially.

Second, a decision will have to be made at the outset concerning the length of time of the strategic planning process itself. In our view, many a strategic planning process has failed because too much time has been devoted to it initially and the planning leader has not enumerated measurable outputs.

If at all possible, give yourself a tight but realistic time frame. Obviously, much of this will depend on the capacity of your organization to expend the person power necessary to complete the planning document as well as juggle the many pressing day-to-day operating issues. We have found, however, that strategic planning processes that are sched-

Phases of the Strategic Planning Process

STEP/TASK	DESCRIPTION
Phase 1: Environmental Assessment	
Phase 2: Ends Planning	
Phase 3: Strategies Planning	
Phase 4: Resource Planning	
Phase 5: Implementation Planning	
Phase 6: Implementation	

Exhibit 2–5   Phases of Strategic Planning Process

uled for more than a nine-to-twelve–month time frame are consumed by their own prodigiousness, fail, and leave their participants even more cynical about the value and outcomes of planning.

Third, your assembled planning team will need to determine whether it can undertake the plan-to-plan or the planning process with in-house personnel, volunteers, or outside expertise. If in-house personnel are utilized, take pains to ensure that the incumbent can and will survive the process, particularly if you are about to engage in a radical approach to mission assessment and program and service delivery. If outside expertise is contemplated, the team must:

- Make sure the outside expert understands, lives, and breathes the nonprofit sector and is passionate about it.
- Ensure that the consultant is objective and not constrained by personal entanglements at the board, volunteer, or staff level.
- Engage only those who are seasoned and who have experienced managing a complex enterprise themselves.

- Understand that you get what you pay for; many times outsiders are willing to do such work pro bono or for radically reduced fees to gain access to the members of the board and the business opportunities they present or the use of the organization's good name as a future reference.

- Thoroughly check references and make sure the chemistry is right. Remember that the organization will be sharing its most intimate of organizational strengths and weaknesses and will need to work with someone who is trustworthy.

Fourth, ascertain what communication mechanisms should be used to announce the plan-to-plan as well as the milestones that are expected to be met throughout the strategic planning process. Also, if you anticipate undertaking a bold new look at your organization or "thinking outside the box," determine what human resources policies should be addressed at the front end. For example, will every incumbent be assured her/his job at the end of the planning process or will incumbents be expected to wear new or different hats? If so, how will they be trained/developed to assume these new functions? Once the plan-to-plan is developed, you will then be in the position to set about the planning process with confidence.

PITFALLS TO AVOID

Strategic planning is both an art and a science. The strategic planning process can take many forms, but we have learned that there are a number of black holes that seem to characterize most planning efforts in the nonprofit sector. What are they and how can you avoid them?

1. The mission inviolate. The mission irrelevant. All too often, board members, volunteers, and staff get "hung up" on the subtleties expressed in the mission statement without asking themselves whether the four elements that should comprise a mission statement actually do exist and are in sync with reality. Concentrate on asking yourself the following soul-searching questions:

- Is the mandate (reason for being) of the organization clearly stipulated?

- Are the values of the organization described in compelling and differentiating terms?

- Has the entity enumerated its aspirations? Is there a cogent statement that articulates not only what the organization currently is but what it wants to become?
- Are the constituents/stakeholders for whom the organization exists identified?

2. *The vision du jour.* We have become almost reverential about the vision stipulated by institutional leaders. All too often, such vision statements appear to change on a daily basis and are so lofty and idealized as not to have any bearing on the entity's capacity to deliver. Remember that a vision statement undergirds or operationalizes the mission of your organization for a period of three to five years through the enumeration of a few select action steps.

CASE STUDY

Defining Mission and Vision for the World's Children

The United States Committee for UNICEF, through Project Redesign, has just adopted a concise mission and vision statement.

I. Mission Statement.
- The U.S. Committee for UNICEF, the United Nations Children's Fund, works for the survival, protection, and development of all children worldwide through education, advocacy, and fund-raising.

II. USC Vision for the Next Three-to-Five Years (Goals)

The U.S. Committee for UNICEF's vision for the next three-to-five years focuses on three target areas:
- education
- advocacy
- fund-raising.

A. **Education**

Goal Statement:
- The U.S. Committee for UNICEF's goal for education is to significantly increase the educational efforts of the organization with the general public, schools, churches, youth groups, volunteers, nongovernmental organizations, and other community partners.

Action Steps:

1. Initiate and implement school-based programs according to plan.

2. Educate staff, volunteers, and the public on UNICEF's mission and goals, including the Convention on the Rights of the Child.

3. Build and develop a nationwide volunteer corp to carry out the education plan.

B. **Advocacy**

Goal Statement:

- The U.S. Committee for UNICEF's advocacy goal is to establish the organization as the principal advocate in the United States for the well-being of all the world's children.

Action Steps:

1. Make advocacy an integral part of the activities, functions, and planning of the U.S. Committee and incorporate advocacy into the education, communications, marketing, and outreach strategies of the organization.

2. Create a network within the organization to disseminate issue and advocacy information, plan and implement policy action initiatives, and generate successful appeals for advocacy action.

3. Train, prepare, and lead the board, staff, volunteers, and donors in advocacy.

4. Serve as both a leader and an active participant in coalitions on issues affecting children, international development, humanitarian relief, and overall foreign assistance policy.

C. **Development (fund-raising)**

Goal Statement:

- The U.S. Committee for UNICEF's development goal is to increase funds raised annually through implementation and/or expansion of such programs as:
  - National UNICEF Month
  - Direct mail
  - Greeting cards, particularly school-based sales
  - Planned giving
  - Other initiatives

- The development goal further is to increase the per capita gift and to lower the cost of raising money in relation to funds actually raised.

Action Steps:

1. Increase direct mail revenue and donor base.
2. Establish major individual donor program.
3. Stimulate the planned giving program.
4. Develop corporate support.
5. Improve the gift acknowledgment process.
6. Decrease the relative direct mail costs.
7. Test new fund-raising projects.
8. Establish a coherent foundation effort.
9. Increase the fund-raising capacity of decentralized offices.
10. Work cooperatively with other USC departments, such as Education, in developing, implementing, and supporting fundraising initiatives.

---

3. Once a member always a member. All too often, volunteers, staff, and others take their constituency for granted. Even more important, those responsible for planning do not explore what its various constituents expect of the organization. Such complacency can be fatal if not consciously addressed. For example, what is the contract or exchange of values an organization must have with its stakeholders or constituents? How solid or tenuous are those relationships and what should be done intentionally to improve them? The generic stakeholder analysis diagrammed in Exhibit 2–6 provides a framework to develop a specific template for your organization.

The most effective way to undertake this exercise is with the planning committee. Leave the circles in the diagram blank and do not ascribe any values to the arrows. Within the larger context of economic, social, demographic, educational, religious, cultural, technological, and political trends, determine the key stakeholders for your organization first. Then, go about a thoughtful and systematic assessment of what a particular constituent wants from your organization in return for what she/he provides. In the case of a volunteer, for example, she/he will provide free labor. In return, the volunteer will sustain her/his relationship with the organization only if she/he feels personal satisfaction or a sense of recognition or self-worth.

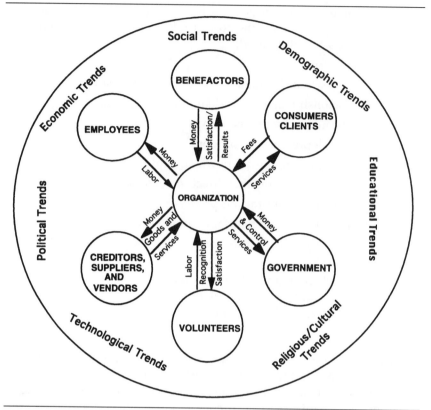

Exhibit 2–6   Stakeholder Analysis

The United Way of America provides an interesting case in point. The organization's new national leadership has had to reconstitute its relationships with donors, large and small, individual or corporate, throughout the country.

CASE STUDY

The United Way of America

From 1982 through 1992, overall corporate giving to charitable causes grew twice as fast as donations to the United Way. Throughout this period, donors became increasingly more likely to donate money directly to specific causes or agencies rather than to the

United Way. During that same period, the number of charities in the United States grew from 320,000 to 500,000, thereby significantly increasing the competition for limited dollars.

It should come as no surprise that these demographics, coupled with the Aramony debacle of 1992, sent the United Way and its member agencies into a tailspin. In 1993, a United Way poll showed that only 3% of respondents were new donors to the United Way, while 40% who had given to the agency in the past decided to pass.

Among the many steps undertaken by the agency's new leadership has been a restructuring of the national board to include more local United Way representation. In April 1995, a twenty-one–member committee of local United Way leaders and members outlined action steps for annual conference participants that permited member charities to raise private donations in the midst of a United Way campaign and redesign the organization's historical message to meet the needs of individuals who work for small business or who are self-employed.

Although the situation described here has been a painful lesson for the United Way and the various charitable entities it supports, we can all learn from it that no one individual or nonprofit organization is above reproach. Indeed, accountability is the rallying cry of the day.

---

4. Be all things to all people. Among the most cogent tidbits we would proffer is "focus, focus, focus." It is no longer possible or wise to attempt to be all things to all people. During the planning process, conscious decision making needs to take place about which programs and services require investment, which need to be maintained, and which need to be divested or eliminated. The grid in Exhibit 2–7 served as a model for the YWCA of the USA as it redesigned the raison d'être of the national office vis-à-vis its community and student associations.

This grid is adopted from investment theory analysis and has wonderful applicability to the nonprofit. Portfolio analysis enables leadership to assess market attractiveness (from high to low) against the strength/relevancy of mission (from high to low). The upper left-hand quadrant (high-high) indicates where a nonprofit should make investments in existing or new programs. In this particular instance, high market attractiveness and strong relevance to mission are compelling reasons to invest.

When a nonprofit has programs with low market attractiveness or demand and the programs are not particularly relevant to the core mission, such programs are primary targets for elimination. Such program elimination/divestment appears in the lower right-hand quadrant of the grid.

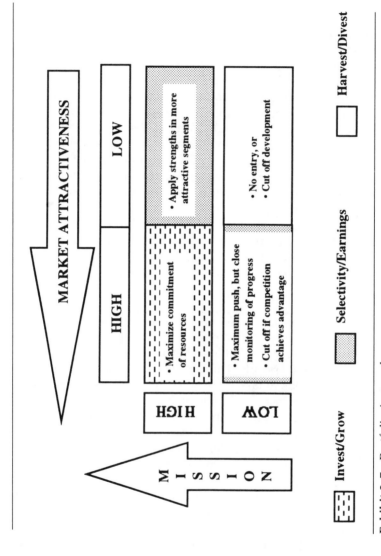

Exhibit 2-7 Portfolio Approach

28

Those programs and services that have low market attractiveness/ demand but are relevant to the mission require prioritizing and the possible reallocation of resources (upper right-hand quadrant). The lower left-hand quadrant contains those programs/services that are not particularly relevant to the mission but have high market attractiveness. In this case, decisions need to be made about continuing such programs and services if peer/competitor organizations draw away clients/program participants.

On the basis of this strategic self-assessment, the YWCA board and the national leadership under the direction of Board President Ann Stallard and Executive Director Dr. Gwendolyn Calvert Baker got the national office out of the provision of direct services and into the businesses of advocacy, research, and fundraising.

5. If we build it, they will come. Frequently nonprofit organizations become complacent. And who can blame them? If you have established an outstanding reputation over the years and are considered best in your class, what is the motivator for change? The answer: the will to change in order to build on competitive strengths and minimize weaknesses.

In our experience, no matter how successful or fragile an organization is, it should focus on those businesses (programs and services) for which it can achieve superior

- *Program differentiation* where its core offerings are unique or highly regarded for their quality;
- *Market focus*, which optimizes service by focusing on specific market segments;
- *Cost position* in price-sensitive markets.

The case study below demonstrates how the leadership of a prestigious institution of higher learning will not rest on its laurels.

CASE STUDY

A Proliferation of Nobel Laureates

For three years in a row, faculty members at the University of Chicago won Nobel Prizes in economics. The social sciences faculty, of which these Nobel laureates are a part, is the envy of many a university president and board of trustees.

Indeed, few other schools provide the rich array of academic offerings and the faculty that the University of Chicago has. In many ways, the academic rigor that has come to characterize the university has emerged as a beacon for world-class scholarship.

Ironically, the university has never been aggressive in marketing itself. Now, with emboldened new leadership and an eye to ever maintaining its international reputation as well as positioning itself in the Greater Chicago area, the university has begun to direct its energies to securing the counsel of public relations consultants.

---

6. Thinking and talking about future wish lists will get us through the tough times. The board and the planning team are often unwilling to make tough decisions. Frequently, strategic planning processes fail because this group is unable to identify the strategies (or the action steps) needed to achieve stipulated goals or to assess the implications each might have on the organization as a whole.

Once again, we have learned that strategic issues must be clearly defined and prioritized. The *Resource Development System* © provides insight into the five criteria by which to judge each element in the strategic plan:

1. *Timing*—Place each strategic issue in order of need and analyze the resources presently available.

2. *Expertise*—Determine whether the issue can be addressed by in-house personnel, volunteers, or consultants in order to acquire the expertise to make it happen.

3. *Revenue*—Determine whether the organization can afford the investment to sustain the issue that is to be implemented.

4. *Constituent needs*—Determine whether the issue will respond to and sustain/encourage constituents and their needs.

5. *Image*—Ask whether the issue will have a positive or negative impact on the entity's image.

INTEGRATED STRATEGIES FOR RESOURCE ALLOCATION

As we have discussed, the strategic plan provides the road map for the organization for a period of three-to-five years. The *operating plan* is designed as the road map for a particular fiscal year within the context of the strategic plan. In essence, the management system enables you to support the objectives enumerated in the strategic plan and should provide the implementation and evaluation criteria for those objectives on an annual basis. Two critical components of the operating plan are the budget and a human resources management plan.

All too often, strategic plans are amorphous and not grounded in the reality of dollars and cents from either the operating or the capital perspective. When strategic plans are linked with the budget or resource allocation process, they often define resource planning from a narrow perspective. But, from our perspective, resource planning (budgeting) should be defined in the most expansive of ways to include

- People (volunteers and staff)
- Operating funds
- Facilities (capital projects planning)
- Equipment

Exhibit 2–8 outlines where resource planning fits into the overall strategic planning process.

A budget is

- An estimated cost of planned activities
- A means of financing
- Expressed in dollars
- A reflection of goals, objectives, and priorities
- Covers a stated period of time

The budget has multiple purposes. It is both a document and a process. As a document, it is a record of the past, a statement of future expectations, and a contract. As a process, the budget is a means of communication, a means of converting rhetoric to action, and a means to arrive at decisions.

The Operating Budget

Depending on the needs and the culture of the organization, resources can be allocated and measured in a number of fundamental ways (see Exhibit 2–9).

A budget has four purposes. The first is its contractual purpose, which enables a manager to control or limit the amount of spending and communicates their budget's limits to those who are responsible for hiring. The most frequently utilized format is the line item budget, which enumerates salaries and benefits of employees, supplies and expenses, and other items.

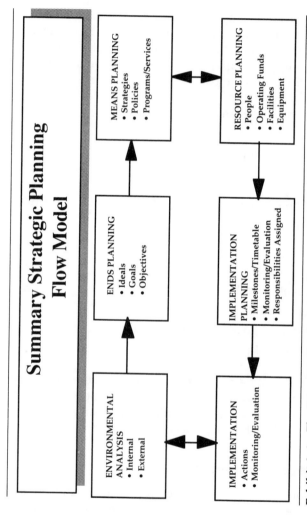

Exhibit 2–8   The Resource Development System

Budgetary Purposes	Format	Focus/Measurement
Control —Limit spending to specific items Communications —Tells how much resources will be used	Line Item	—Input —Economy Measures
Contract —What work will be performed and at what cost Management Tool —Provide information that allows manager to assess efficiency Communication —Provides information as to what is being performed	Performance	—Process/Output —Efficiency Measures Workload Unit Cost
Planning —Identifies goals and objectives to be achieved Policy —Allows choice between policy goals and between alternative means of reaching goals Communication —Shows purpose of expenditures and the policies and priorities of the institution	Program	—Outcomes/Impact —Effectiveness Measures
Policy —Allows choices between different levels of output associated with each functioning level	Zero Base	—Output: Workload Unit Cost —Input: Cost

Exhibit 2–9 Budget Purpose and Format

Another purpose for a budget is to establish a contract that stipulates what a particular division or unit will do and at what cost. From this perspective it serves as a management and communication tool for performance measurement with the focus on process and such efficiency measures as unit costs and workload.

A third purpose of a budget is to focus on planning, which takes a longer term view and looks at the programs your organization offers. For each program identified, the manager stipulates the goals and objectives to be achieved and enumerates the different ways in which they can be achieved, as well as the outcomes anticipated for each proposed expenditure.

The fourth purpose of a budget is to achieve fundamental redefinition of mission and/or policy. If this is the case, zero-base budgeting is the approach to embrace. Although time consuming and anxiety provoking, it can provide some very helpful insights about how and why you are allocating your organization's resources the way you are. In such an approach, each manager is asked to justify the existence of her/his unit from a base of zero or the ground up. In such a scenario, programs and services are defined, and costs are allocated to those programs and services, which are then rank ordered in importance to the unit. Both outputs (workload and unit costs) and inputs (the direct and indirect costs of providing programs and services) are measured.

In addition to these four basic approaches, growing numbers of executive directors and their boards are attempting to develop new models to empower staff to generate and manage resources at levels throughout the organization. These incentive-based models can be traced to the concept of *intramural funding* (developed by Daniel D. Robinson and Frederick J. Turk and others), designed to distribute resources among separate but related entities. Such incentive-based models require that senior management make decisions regarding the assignment of revenues and expenditures to a particular program, department or service. A disciplined approach which incorporates the following questions must be undertaken:

1. Certain revenues and expenditures directly result from the activities of a particular program, department, or service.

   Question: Should they be assigned?

   - Completely
   - Partially
   - Not at all

2. Certain revenues and expenditures benefit the entire organization.

   Question: Should they be allocated?

- Completely
- Partially
- Not at all

Depending on the answers to these queries, managers can determine whether to take one of four budgeting approaches:

- Cost center approach
- Profit center approach (primary programs)
- Profit center approach (all programs)
- Full absorption

The cost center approach holds managers responsible for living within the budget they have been allocated and does not hold them accountable for generating revenues to offset expenses. This, rather, is the responsibility of those senior managers who are responsible for fund raising, development, and grantsmanship. A profit center approach, on the other hand, holds the program director or unit head responsible not only for luring within the budget allocation but also for generating an excess of revenues over expenditures or a profit through fund raising, program fees, grantsmanship, etc. A full absorption model requires that the unit head function, in essence, as the chief executive of her/his division; that is, all costs both direct and indirect, are assigned to the unit head's budget as are the revenues generated.

Given today's thrust of assigning authority and responsibility to the lowest levels of the organization, the schematic in Exhibit 2–10 should enable you to determine the wisdom and practicality of adopting an incentive-based resource allocation model for your organization, which permits managers to make decisions that will ensure that resources are being utilized in the most efficient and cost effective manner possible. In our experience, if you are not willing to develop and implement a merit/incentive-based compensation system or if you are not willing or able (because of federal or state mandates) to allow managers to carry forward funds from one operating year to the next, this incentive-based reallocation model is *not* for you or your organization.

The Capital Budget

So far, we have focused on the operating budget. For many nonprofit managers, the capital budget is simply out of their reach because such

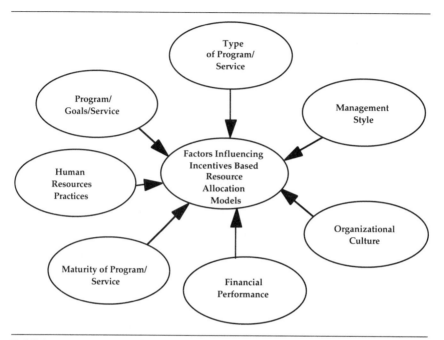

Exhibit 2–10   Factors Influencing Incentive-based Allocation Models

responsibility is lodged with the vice president for finance and administration and/or a subcommittee of the board. Consequently, there is little or no direct input or discussion between those who control the purse strings and the staff whose lives are greatly influenced by the purchase and ongoing upgrade of a personal computer or freshly painted office walls in a well-maintained building.

Simply put, a *capital budget* is a plan that identifies the major asset items that have been assigned a high priority for purchase and delineates their funding source. All too often, capital budgets are not linked to the strategic plan, in large measure because managers often view capital expenditures as distinct from programmatic and/or service priorities.

The tenuous financial condition of many entities has further exacerbated this separation of strategic planning from capital budgeting and has led to the shelving of capital construction projects and the purchase of equipment. We see this situation concretely manifested in the all-too-common laundry list of deferred maintenance projects and the scattershot approach of assigning personal computers to staff at many nonprofits.

We have learned that the following three principles must be at work in developing the capital budget:

1. Well-planned capital decisions contribute to fulfilling long-range and strategic goals.
2. Capital acquisition priorities must be guided by the strategic plan.
3. The process must have a multiyear horizon.

Capital and operating budgets are differentiated by four elements: the nature of the items purchased, the benefits accrued, the methods of financing, and the decision-making process utilized (see Exhibit 2–11).

Specifically, capital funding sources include operating income, debt, capital campaigns or fund drives, investment income, proceeds from the sale of assets, and funded depreciation.

In determining when capital expenditures should be made to support the strategic plan, the following decision criteria should be utilized:

- Safety
- Federal and state requirements
- Equipment replacement schedule
- Preventive maintenance schedule

Element	Operating Budget	Capital Budget
1. Nature of Items Purchased	• Depleted Within One Year	• Long-Term Benefit • Useful Life Span • Physical Presence • Expensive
2. Benefits	• Current Period	• Future Periods
3. Methods of Financing	• Current Funds	• Plant Funds Restricted Unrestricted • Current Fund Transfers • Other Sources
4. Decision Making	• Often Incremental • Influenced by Key Behavioral Variables	• More Prone to Quantitative Analysis

Exhibit 2–11 Operating and Capital Budgets

- Revenue production
- Cost reduction
- New program or service requirement
- Program or service improvement
- Operating maintenance requirements

Human Resources

As most operating budgets in the nonprofit sector predominantly involve people costs, it is critical that a human resources plan be explicitly enumerated as part of strategic planning and resources allocation. For most nonprofit organizations, for example, people costs range from 70 percent to 80 percent of the institution's operating budget. Contrast this with approximately 6 percent to 10 percent of the operating budget of a manufacturing firm.

Ironically, nonprofit organizations pay little attention to developing an intentional set of activities to ensure that their human resources are being used in the most effective and efficient manner. We recommend that the following human resource systems/procedures be in place to support the operating plan:

- *Maintain a current organization chart* that enumerates reporting relationships and functions.
- *Maintain position descriptions* for each position that list responsibilities in detail.
- *Use performance evaluations* to communicate to staff how well they are performing and whether responsibilities are being handled optimally.
- *Establish merit incentive programs* to determine and explain how and why salary increases are made.
- *Invest time and dollars in training and development* to build staff skills. How is your staff encouraged/assisted in embracing new technologies?

We recommend that once you operationalize such a human resources plan as part of the strategic planning process for the paid staff that the same be undertaken for your organization's directors and volunteers.

In Chapter 6, we will focus our discussion further on maximizing staff and volunteer resources.

THE NEED TO KNOW

One of the classic challenges facing executive directors and their boards is the degree to which strategic planning and resource allocation should be shared with the organization's various constituents. Although we philosophically espouse that such information needs to be shared to the greatest extent possible, we believe that care must be taken to discern the difference (and, therefore, the level of detail) between making high-level policy decisions and having responsibility for day-to-day implementation.

The strategic resource management pyramid depicted in Exhibit 2–12 is an attempt to help you discern, for example, what should be shared with the board and with senior management, directors, and department heads.

MONITORING THE STRATEGIC PLAN

Whereas the organization's management team utilizes the operating plan to assess day-to-day progress on a fiscal-year basis, the board in partnership with the executive director must monitor the longer term (three-to-five–year) activities that comprise the strategic plan.

The methodology for assessing the strategic plan should reflect the plan's particular design. If, for example, the strategic plan format is based on functional lines, the evaluation should be conducted in a parallel manner. If the plan's format is focused on strategic issues or strategic action steps, the evaluation should be conducted in that manner.

Much to its credit, The Johns Hopkins University has intentionally developed a planning process with a built-in monitoring system university-wide.

CASE STUDY

Creating an Interactive Institution

In September 1994, The Johns Hopkins University published its *Report of the Committee for the 21st Century*. The committee was chartered by President William C. Richardson and Provost Joseph Cooper to "examine critically and imaginatively every aspect of the University's organization and programs in order to recommend ways in which Johns Hopkins can remain at the forefront of higher education through the year 2000 and beyond."

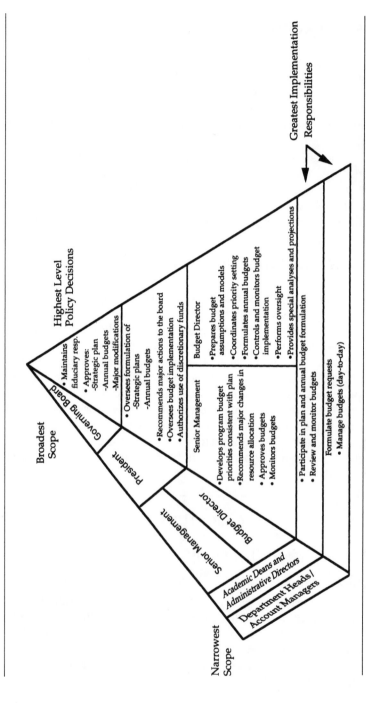

Exhibit 2-12 Strategic Resource Management Pyramid

Broadest Scope

Highest Level Policy Decisions

Governing Board
- Maintains fiduciary resp.
- Approves:
  - Strategic plan
  - Annual budgets
  - Major modifications

President
- Oversees formulation of
  - Strategic plans
  - Annual budgets
- Recommends major actions to the board
- Oversees budget implementation
- Authorizes use of discretionary funds

Senior Management
- Develops program budget priorities consistent with plan
- Recommends major changes in resource allocation
- Approves budgets
- Monitors budgets

Budget Director
- Prepares budget assumptions and models
- Coordinates priority setting
- Formulates annual budgets
- Controls and monitors budget implementation
- Performs oversight
- Provides special analyses and projections

Academic Deans and Administrative Directors
- Participate in plan and annual budget formulation
- Review and monitor budgets

Department Heads / Account Managers
- Formulate budget requests
- Manage budgets (day-to-day)

Narrowest Scope

Greatest Implementation Responsibilities

40

The vision of the committee was to create "an interactive institution, broadly connected externally, and highly focused and collaborative internally." Eight institutional imperatives and twenty-three specific recommendations were enumerated. The imperatives included

Increasing collaboration

Sharpening institutional focus

Improving the information infrastructure

Expanding international dimensions

Enhancing the undergraduate program

Increasing attention to community and citizenship

Enhancing institutional effectiveness and efficiency

Securing the university's financial future

The Provost indicates that eight strategic study groups, comprised predominantly of faculty, developed these powerful, cross-institutional imperatives and have been charged with the ongoing implementation and evaluation of these imperatives. Their findings will enable the president and the provost to report progress on a regular basis to the board of trustees, the alumni, the university staff and faculty, as well as a myriad of external constituents.

Such systematic evaluation, if properly designed, should be able to answer the following questions:

- Did we really accomplish what we said we would?
- So what?
- Now what?

There are three general purposes to evaluation mechanisms:

1. To measure progress
2. To establish criteria for success or best practices
3. To provide ongoing and systematic input for the plan

The Johns Hopkins example shows a cross-functional approach to strategic planning and evaluation. The National Wildlife Federation case study demonstrates the way in which that organization imposed discipline through the *Resource Development System* © to evaluate its programs and services on a continuous basis.

CASE STUDY

Building a Continuous Evaluation Process

In 1990, the National Wildlife Federation, under the direction of Dr. Jay Haire, president and CEO, embraced the fundamental tenets of the *Resource Development System* © (RDS), a "process to develop effective plans, orchestrate resources, diversify revenue, and motivate constituents." The RDS process involves five steps:

Step One: The Resource Audit

- Organizational Audit
  - Mission
  - Program/Services
  - Environment
  - Structure
  - Operations
- Functional Audit
  - Constituency Development
  - Marketing
  - Communications
  - Revenue Generation

Step Two: The Strategic Plan

Step Three: The Operating Plan

Step Four: Implementation

Step Five: Evaluation

For each of the following five years, Dr. Haire and his senior managers evaluated progress utilizing the teams established to prepare the RDS plans. For example, they assessed their retail operations, the educational programs they offer K-12 students, their fundraising and development operations, and so on. Dr. Haire reported that the RDS, which they modified to serve their own organizational needs and a complex mix of programs, services, and retail operations, enabled the board, the staff, and their volunteer structures to determine and focus on the needs of their constituencies on a consistent basis.

KEYS TO SUCCESSFUL PLANNING

When you design a strategic planning and resource allocation process for your organization, be sure that the following attributes are present:

- Ends-oriented, means-secondary orientation: What do we ultimately want to accomplish? How do we get there?
- Holistic, systems oriented: Are we looking at the whole? Do we understand that if we change one aspect of our program/service delivery mechanism that the entire organization will be affected?
- Participative structure: Have we included key employees and volunteers in the process?
- Continuous action: How do we ensure that the plan does not become a shelf document?
- Valuing of both experience and experiment: How do we ensure our core values will be there at the end of the process while asking the tough questions?
- Ideal seeking but realistic: How can we dream but be pragmatic at the same time?
- Realistic time horizon for intermediate objectives and goals: How do we make sure that we can accomplish our goals and objectives within an idealistic time frame?
- Linking of plans to resources (budget): How do we develop a strategic planning process that has a resource allocation component/budget? Is the timing of both in sync with our organization's fiscal year?
- Fixes responsibility for the development, implementation and monitoring of the process—who will be accountable at every step of the process?
- Is completed early—how do we ensure that the constituents who need to participate have the time to make thoughtful decisions?

- Has capacity to encumber the cast of goods purchased before actual payment of the goods—do we have the systems in place to monitor our budget on a timely and accurate basis?

- Has capacity to carry-forward an operating surplus—does our organization have the interest in providing incentives to management and volunteers?

- Relies on quantitative data and techniques but also on subjective judgment and values: When is too much data, too much? When/how should we trust our gut instincts?

- Integrates overall organization objectives and policies with departmental/divisional operating objectives and policies: How do we ensure that our charity's overarching goals and objectives are part of departmental/divisional goals and objectives?

- Seeks to align organizational and individual (staff and volunteer) goals by creating appropriate incentives and rewards: How can we create a resource allocation/budget process that provides incentives for prudent fiscal management? Is there a way in which we can create an employee performance measurement system that motivates the behavior/culture we want to generate?

- Seeks to shape the future, not merely to survive or avoid it: How can we muster the will to do the right things? Get ahead of trends? Create a distinctive/distinguishing future?

Given what we have learned from your colleagues, we offer a generic strategic planning and resource allocation model for your consideration in Exhibit 2–13. The horizontal axis indicates the nine stages that comprise the strategic planning and resource allocation process. The vertical axis stipulates the organizational level at which the various steps of each stage of the process should occur. The organizational level starts with the board/CEO and proceeds through the customers or constituents.

Each of the numbered circles indicates the sequential order in which each step should be undertaken and at what level in the organization. The process ebbs and flows as is indicated in the exhibit. You will need to adapt the stages of the process and the organizational level at which the various steps occur to address the particular culture of your organization and the needs your own groups have for the strategic planning and resource allocation process.

The first step of Stage 1 of the process begins at the board/CEO level and focuses on creating/affirming an organization-wide mission and vision. Division heads are asked to provide their input to the board and CEO for their review and analysis (Step 3). The next step in the process

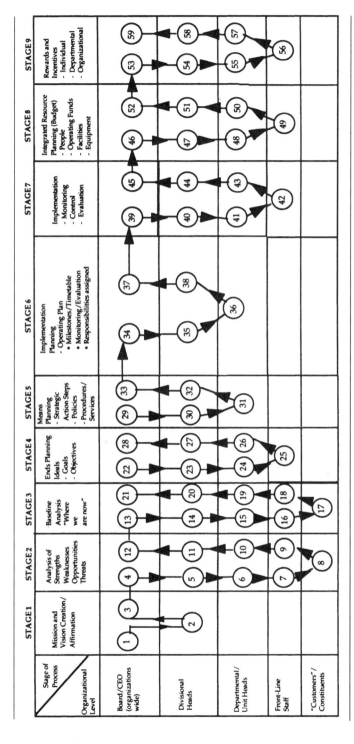

Exhibit 2–13   Strategic Planning and Resource Allocation Process

45

(Step 4) commences Stage 2, the analysis of organizational strengths, weaknesses, opportunities, and threats. In Stage 2, every constituent group participates, both reacting to what is provided to them by another constituency or manager and, in turn, conducting analyses of their own, responding to what was provided them and forwarding that analysis up to the next level within the organization. The process goes along accordingly.

For purposes of this exhibit, there are fifty-nine steps. Stage 9, Rewards and Incentives, depicts the culmination of one complete cycle of the strategic planning and resource allocation process. It demonstrates the depth of the individual, departmental, and organizational reward and incentive systems and procedures.

If you are clear about where you and your organization are going, you are then in the position to think boldly about whether your organization is supporting its mission and its constituents in the most optimal manner. For those who have the constitutional fortitude and will, reengineering is the next step.

CHAPTER THREE

Restructuring and Reengineering Your Nonprofit

Ｈow many times have you heard a well-intentioned board member exclaim: "I know it will be painful, but we must learn to do more with less. So many people are depending on us, and we can't let them down."

Such exclamations of commitment and frustration are increasing in number daily in the nonprofit sector. Yet, how realistic, *truly realistic*, is it to assume that staff and volunteers can wear many more hats? In our view, *to do more with less* at this turn of the millennium is an impossibility.

What then are the available solutions to the vexing conundrum of the escalating need for programs and services and the decline and competition for philanthropic resources? Obviously, there is no one simple answer. Many organizations have responded with across-the-board or straight percentage budget cuts. In recent years, others have begun to use some of the fundamental tenets of the continuous quality improvement movement and reengineering, embracing them as opportunities for targeted and in-depth transformation rather than superficial change.

What differentiates those who choose the across-the-board solution from those who choose the restructuring and reengineering solution? The answer is **WILL**.

Simply put, reengineering is not for the faint of heart. It requires enormous risk taking, confidence, trust, willing leaders and followers, and perhaps most important, the willingness to admit when mistakes are made, to learn from them, and to go forward with renewed strength and self-confidence.

SUSTAINING THE CARE-GIVING CULTURE IN A TIME OF PROFOUND CHANGE

Perhaps the greatest obstacle to change in a nonprofit organization is its pervasive goal of providing care, programs, and services to those in need under any circumstance. The powerful mission statements and their accompanying good works pose a daunting challenge to change for executive directors and board members alike.

In contrast with the for-profit sector and the health care market segment of the nonprofit sector, which was forced into fundamental redesign over a decade ago in order to survive, only in recent memory have other nonprofits begun to redesign themselves. Among the drivers for change are the following:

- The current challenge from the American public and its elected representatives to the impressive legacy of the nonprofit sector on both the local and the national levels regarding its accountability to the public.

- The ability of the nonprofit sector to maintain current service levels and programs not necessarily found in the for-profit sector.

- The increased attention of accreditation, affiliation, and certification processes to address the tough business decisions these organizations must make to survive (particularly in K-12 and post–secondary education and health care).

- An acknowledgment and appreciation of the need for better training for nonprofit leaders/managers.

- Soul-searching governance reviews that question the wisdom of securing and retaining board members who may have sought identification with the organization more for business connections or social prestige than for the duties of stewardship and public trust.

How can the sector balance the provision of good works and the delivery of professionally recognized programs and services while remaining true to its mission and being open to change? The answer lies in part in a thorough understanding of the history of the nonprofit sector as a whole and of the culture of the individual market segments and organizations themselves. Health care providers, performing arts organizations, social services organizations, and colleges and universities have collectively and individually evolved through history and precedent. As such, each has its own unique attributes. Over time, these organizations have created their own mechanisms for control and accountability, in the form of internal controls, sign-offs, auditing, accrediting agencies, and the like. For example, many nonprofit organizations require that the staff person requesting that paper and other office supplies be purchased for his department get written approval for such a purchase order at the manager and/or vice president level before the purchase can be authorized. These procedures have historically provided the controls and accountability that are perceived to be important in keeping people honest and complying with standard operating procedures.

INTERNAL FOCUS

Perhaps one of the most salient characteristics of the nonprofit sector is its turf-driven mentality. How many times have you heard or even expressed the following divisions yourself:

For performing arts organizations: The artistic side of the house; the managerial side of the house.

For museums: The curatorial/research side of the house; the administrative/financial side of the house.

For social services agencies: The program side of the house; the financial side of the house.

For colleges and universities: The academic side of the house; the administrative/financial side of the house.

Turf comes at a price—a price many organizations can no longer afford. Not only does it create communication and relational problems; it also necessarily creates the demand and sustenance of a cadre of relatively highly paid specialists. Examples include grants accountants, budget analysts, information technology specialists, and cost analysts. This, in turn, leads to fragmentation and duplication of administrative support activities across the organization and layers and layers of unnecessary cost.

Organizations evolve around people—the skills they bring, their relationships with significant power brokers, and their institutional memories. A look at any organization chart will yield numerous staffing and reporting anomalies resulting in large measure from the personal relationships incumbents have established and maintained with those in power. This power aura limits the capacity of an organization to be flexible and to change.

The turf and personality-driven attributes just described yield an internally focused and costly infrastructure. Worse, these attributes reinforce one other in such a manner as to create a series of vertically driven structures ("silos" or "stovepipes" in management jargon) which are *sui generis* in nature. Whereas communication and decision making are hierarchical in this kind of culture, they are seldom witnessed across the silos. For example, in many colleges and universities, decisions regarding a change in an individual faculty member's workload are not always routinely supplied to the registrar who is responsible for class scheduling. This creates scheduling problems not only for the individual faculty member but the students enrolled in that class as well. In another example, a childcare classroom that has been converted to a teacher's lounge and is no longer available for teaching three-year-olds is summarily removed from the classroom inventory by the master teacher, but the teacher who is responsible for that particular class of three-year-olds is not informed.

Although such structures and the culture they breed provide serene comfort to those who want a clearly defined job in a clearly defined space, they are not the structures and attributes that will sustain the nonprofit for the long haul. As described in Chapter 2, the future demands that the nonprofit sector embrace even more strongly its mission-based and constituency-driven nature. This means that individual organizations and their leaders will have to actualize their visions and empower staff and volunteers to do their part. Each entity will need to emerge as externally focused, efficient, and responsive. In short, volunteers and staff alike must be willing to make the investment to redesign themselves from a hierarchically driven model that is all too internally focused to a service-oriented organization that is more consciously driven by the market (its constituents).

Exhibit 3–1 graphically depicts the change from a traditional, hierarchical organization to one that functions interactively and vests authority, responsibility, and accountability at every level of the organization. In the traditional organization, managers function within their own organizational walls or turf. Communication and decision making flow from the top of the organization down to the lowest levels of the organization, and decisions are communicated across the boundaries or turf. Each of the units/divisions functions as if it were an independent body not part of the entire organization. The empowered, interactive organization on the other hand, has fewer levels of bureaucracy. Its structure is relatively flat, thus enabling communication to occur more readily and comfortably across the organization. Additionally, people who are responsible for the management of key adminstrative processes and programs are part of the decision-making process as change occurs.

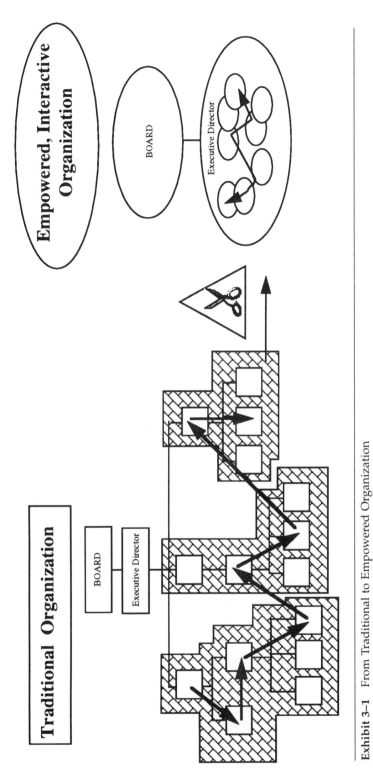

Exhibit 3–1 From Traditional to Empowered Organization

Source: Alceste T. Pappas, Ph.D., © Pappas Consulting Group, Inc.

1. The mission statement is inviolate.

2. Every major policy and operating decision must emanate from and relate directly to the mission statement.

3. The executive director and the board must share a vision that stipulates clearly three to five action steps that support the mission to be accomplished in the short term.

4. Constituents (be they students, clients, donors, volunteers) are the primary reason for the organization's existence.

5. The role of the staff (and the faculty if an educational institution) is to create and support a learning and nurturing environment that enables the generation of new knowledge, the provision of programs and services, and/or advocacy.

6. Staff and volunteers exist to enable constituents to succeed in accomplishing their individual and collective missions.

7. Constituents external to the organization provide a reality check and serve as institutional stakeholders.

8. Authority and accountability must be vested with everyone, including the board, staff, and external constituents.

Exhibit 3-2   The Pappas Principles
Source: The Will to Transform the Academic Core, Alceste T. Pappas, Ph.D., © Pappas Consulting Group Inc.

DEFINING THE PRINCIPLES OF CHANGE

Before embarking on reengineering, you need to define the principles upon which you will guide your efforts. In our experience, there are eight principles that provide the underpinnings for success (see Exhibit 3–2). These will have emerged in the strategic planning efforts you undertook as the precursor to reengineering. You will want to tailor these generic principles to fit the unique needs of your organization. Drake University, a private institution in the Mid-West has done such tailoring to fit its unique culture.

CASE STUDY

Taking the Plunge: Defining Reengineering Criteria

On November 18, 1994, Duke University's Steering Committee for Work Redesign presented a list of criteria that would serve as the basis for its reengineering efforts. The criteria were

Mission critical process

Not mission critical; an opportunity for learning

Impact of process/number of customers served

Fits the systems (e.g., client server)

Dissatisfaction with the process

Clear benchmarks for cost savings

Availability of resources (number of available staff members)

Potentially probable acceptance of the change by key constituents

During the course of their discussion, members of the Steering Committee posted three additional criteria: (1) empower employees; (2) generate immediate payback/results; and (3) enable people to focus primarily on their job and not on administrative trivia.

The case of the National office of the YWCA of the USA points out how the executive director and her board defined the specific guidelines that would lead to a redesigned organization.

CASE STUDY

Establishing Reengineering Guidelines for a Venerable Women's Movement

Dr. Gwendolyn Calvert Baker talks about establishing guidelines for reengineering the National Office of the YWCA of the USA in *Redesigning the Nonprofit Organization: How Vision, Leadership, and Planning Helped One Nonprofit Redefine Itself* (Washington, DC: National Center for Nonprofit Governing Boards, 1993 pp. 4–5). Dr. Baker's work contains some striking similarities, to the case of Duke University and the Pappas Principles enumerated in Exhibit 3–2:

Our first action was to establish guidelines for the reengineering project. At that time, the board leadership and I believed that the project would have more of a chance of success if the planning process were directed through a set of guidelines that all participants could accept. Thus, we adopted the following guidelines:

1. **The project would have well-defined goals**. Our goals were to redesign the national office to become more effective, more efficient, and more relevant to the mission and to reduce costs.

2. **The project would be mission-driven**. The mission of the YWCA would be used as the driving force and thus would ensure an objective decision-making process.

3. **The redesign process would be inclusive and interactive**. To succeed, the redesign effort required the support of the governing bodies, national office staff, and the volunteers and staffs of the local YWCAs. All of these groups would be consulted and included; their participation was key to ensuring legitimacy and ownership.

4. **All decisions would be based on research**. To ensure legitimacy and objectivity, all decisions would be made based on research rather than anecdote or instinct.

5. **Open communications would be maintained throughout the project**. All study participants would be regularly informed about the direction and the progress of the project.

6. **The project would be conducted with professional assistance**. The process required guidance and expertise not available within the YWCA. The participation of a consulting firm was critical.

These case studies of two different sectors within the nonprofit marketplace underscore the need to ask yourself and your organization the following soul-searching questions:

- Where do we want to start and where do we want to end up?

- What do our constituents want and expect from us? How driven by constituent needs and wants should our organization be?

- What are the key processes that influence our various internal and external constituents?

- Is there enough pain within our organization to drive change? Do we possess the will to change? Do we have people in-house who are capable of being change enablers?

- How must we go about implementing change in our organization so that our endeavors will succeed?

THE FUNDAMENTAL COMPONENTS OF CHANGE

In essence, reengineering is a balanced approach to maximizing organizational effectiveness and efficiency that incorporates the tenets of right sizing, restructuring, Total Quality Management/Continuous Quality Improvement (TQM/CQI), and automation/technology breakthroughs. Exhibit 3–3 illustrates the three critical components of process redesign or reengineering. The first is organization, including structure, culture, and the ways in which performance is measured on an individual volunteer or staff basis and on a departmental, unit, or division basis. The second critical component is systems and technology. More specifically, software, hardware, networks, and telecommunications are all essential elements to process redesign and help to provide the infrastructure to ensure that work gets done right the first time. A third critical component includes workflow, policies, procedures, facilities, and equipment. It is sometimes simpler, for example, to maximize service delivery by changing a staff member's reporting relationship rather than where his/her office should be.

Proponents of reengineering use that word in a myriad of ways to describe a full range of management improvements. What truly makes an "improvement" program reengineering? In our view, the best succinct definition is to be found in AMACOM's 1994 publication, *The Reengineering Handbook*:

> Reengineering is the rapid and radical redesign of strategic, value-added business processes—and the systems, policies and organizational structures that support them—to optimize the work flows and productivity in an organization.

To better understand this definition of reengineering, let's examine the meaning of the key operative words in this paragraph.

Key Operative Term	Definition
• Rapid	• Produces results quickly
• Radical redesign (performance breakthrough)	• Creating a totally new approach, one that flies in the face of conventional wisdom
• Strategic	• Central to the company's raison d'être
• Value-added	• Provides the customer with what he/she expects/needs/is willing to pay for

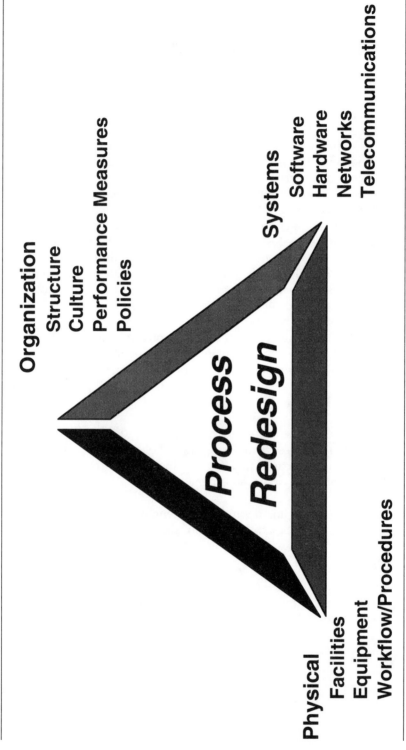

Exhibit 3–3   Components of Process Redesign

• Processes	• An interrelated series of activities that converts inputs into outputs (e.g., recruiting a new staff member is an input; putting that new staff member on payroll is an output)
• Systems, policies, and organizations	• The support infrastructure for process flows or the ways in which things move through the system/organization
• Optimize work flows and productivity	• Increase profitability, market share, revenue, return-on-investment, equity, or assets

The definition just presented comes from corporate literature and focuses on the business processes that comprise the for-profit entities. Such business processes include purchasing, accounts payable, accounts receivable, travel reimbursement, payroll processing, and the like.

How can reengineering be defined for the nonprofit sector, given its mission-based and constituency-driven culture? We offer the following altered definition:

> Reengineering is the redesign of strategic, value-added processes—and the systems, policies, and organizational structures that support them—to optimize service and program delivery as well as productivity.

Again, we suggest breaking apart this definition into its component parts.

Key Operative Term	**Definition**
• Processes	• An interrelated series of activities that converts inputs into outcomes (e.g., recruiting a new staff member)
• Value-added	• Provides the constituent with a service/program/education that increases his/her benefit over a period of time
• Strategic	• Central to the entity's mission and vision

- Systems, policies, and organizational structures

- The supporting infrastructure for the process (e.g., programs, services, learning, administration)

- Optimize service and program delivery

- Generates long-term outcomes, constituent satisfaction, and excess of revenues over expenditures (profit) to invest in mission and future of organization; provides seamless service, one-stop shopping

Reengineering purists could argue that the definition we provided does not constitute reengineering because it does not espouse rapid change. In our experience, one of the very defining and salient characteristics of the nonprofit sector is its outcome rather than output-driven culture.

For example, it takes at least seven to eight years to generate a Ph.D. in history. It takes months and on-going follow-up for a Hazelden alumnus to stay clean of a codependency on drugs and alcohol. This is a sector, unlike its corporate counterpart, that provides long-term (longitudinal) outcomes rather than an instant product, such as a pair of new Nike running shoes or a Lexus straight off the assembly line.

Further, it is a sector that is rather resilient. We confess this is both a boon and a bane. As this industry is truly based on mission and is driven by its constituents, it is considerably more resilient to the vicissitudes of change and in many ways is in the enviable position of being more protected and sacred than its for-profit counterparts.

THE ROLE OF TECHNOLOGY IN REENGINEERING

As nonprofits become increasingly computer literate, they must be deliberate about what they want that technology to accomplish. How can technology make a difference in delivering core mission programs and services? Experience has taught us that the principles of reengineering need to be applied to the individual at a computer terminal, be it volunteer or staff member.

With the growing number of personal computers on the desks of volunteers and staff and the advancements in client server technology, the role of the user as knowledge worker is key. No longer are computers primarily for data entry. Rather, and more important, they serve as enablers to those who need to translate data into information and ultimately into knowledge so that they can fulfill their role in the organization. As a consequence, you need to develop guidelines to assess individual staff and volunteer activity, as well as group or team productivity.

Productivity

Here are some questions that should be asked to assess individual productivity:

- What are the differences between the person's real and defined job description?
- What should this person ideally be doing?
- Can technology be helpful to the incumbent?
- What can the individual and the organization as a whole expect in return for this investment in technology?
- How will we be able to measure any gains in productivity?
- Will the incumbent's role change after automation?

Here are some of the questions that should be routinely asked while assessing group or team productivity. This is not an ad hoc process, but rather an ongoing one:

- With whom do team members routinely interact?
- What is the team's function?
- What technology currently supports the team's work?
- How can administrative processes and the delivery of services be improved through investment in new technology?
- How can process improvement be measured?
- Will the team need to continue in its current form after automation has been completed and process redesign has been accomplished?

Guidelines for New Technology Strategies

Executive directors and their boards should use a set of guidelines to assess their organization's strategic technology plan no matter what the degree of automation. Here are some valuable lessons that we have gleaned from the experiences of your colleagues.

1. The mission of most nonprofits is borne of the creation and dissemination of knowledge. To that end, you must recognize that this fact is critical to both the short- and long-term success of your organization. Your organization does not need information technology that will work miracles, but it does need technology to serve as an enabler of process redesign.

2. You will never be able to arrive at an exact price tag for your technology investment. In many ways, technology investments require leaps of faith as they constitute both measurable and subjective elements as communications infrastructures and executive support systems.

3. Not all technological advances will work, so you need to be initially sanguine about which advancements should be ignored, which should be watched with skepticism, and which should be implemented head-on. If you have done your homework and have a strong sense of institutional purpose, you should be able to make the right investment decisions.

4. Technology and related infrastructure investments are for the long term. Do not expect immediate gratification. Be sure to communicate this most basic fact of life to your constituents.

5. Be sure to recruit or garner access (through a management contract) to the very best technology experts. Such experts need not only have the requisite technical skills; they also need to have excellent communication, listening, coaching, and teaching skills.

6. You must appoint the most competent project manager you can find, one who has the respect and trust of your multiple constituencies and one who is a master of change management. Further, you must share your own personal conviction that the technology will simply not function by itself or in isolation, but rather in an integrated network across the nonprofit.

7. Most fundamentally, technology is not a panacea. It is merely the enabler for fundamental change in the organization. Senior leadership, therefore, has the responsibility (both the staff and the volunteers) to develop the broad vision for technology in support of the overall organization's mission and vision.

Reengineering requires the development of a strategic technology plan to enable changes in administrative processes to become a reality. Although any discussion about technology is only as timely as the day it was written, there are some far-reaching changes that are revolutionizing the fundamental manner in which we communicate with one other and make decisions. Two changes will have profound impact on our organizations for decades to come: The first is client server technology; and the second is groupware.

Client-Server Technology

What is client-server technology? Client-server technology allows you to distribute the processing of data between a client (user) with a front-end device such as a personal computer or terminal and a server or back-end processor. In such a scenario, the user is responsible for the user interface and data validation functions, while the server handles the data repository functions. Client-server architecture can be very complex, integrating various technologies and inculcating profound cultural, behavioral, and technical changes among users and information technology specialists. In essence, such a client (user)-server approach represents a shift from data center control and management to user control and systems management as it is the user who defines his/her data and information needs.

If, after intensive self-assessment and reengineering, you are willing to consider integrating client-server technology in your nonprofit, heed the lessons from a recent study conducted by Sidney Diamond of fifty corporate CIOs (adapted from Sidney Diamond, "The Wild West of Corporate Computing," *Financial Executive*, March/April 1995, pp. 43–46):

- Client-server technology is *not* the equivalent of a local area network (LAN) operating system.
- A growing number of mainframe application developers are adapting to the client-server environment.
- Be patient. It will take some time for client-server applications to be readily available to the nonprofit world at large.
- The client-server environment is a challenge to implement because end users need to be trained and be provided the technical support to run the production systems.
- There are challenges to data security for the end users.
- Initially, client-server technology will not save resources. It requires considerable hardware, software, and training costs; however, the benefits to streamlining operations and empowering employees are tremendous.

Groupware

Groupware is personal computer (PC) software that combines a sophisticated messaging system with a large database containing work records and memos. Such software changes the manner in which information flows throughout your organization by creating a nonprofit on-line service. Such software compels organizations to question their current modus operandi and reengineer. As David Kirkpatrick describes in the December 27, 1993, issue of *Fortune* in "Groupware Goes Boom":

> By giving workers well below the top of the organizational pyramid access to information previously unavailable or restricted to upper levels of management, groupware spreads power far more widely than before. Many who have grown comfortable dealing near the pyramid's apex are understandably distressed by the way groupware disrupts old style hierarchies. (p. 99)

REENGINEERING: REVOLUTION OR EVOLUTION FOR THE NONPROFIT?

In the December 13, 1993, issue of *Fortune* magazine, Thomas A. Stewart wrote an article with a heart-stopping title, "Welcome to the Revolution." The opening paragraphs of this compelling story say:

> In a historic convergence, not one but four business revolutions are upon us. For your future, embrace them:
> Let us not use the word cheaply. Revolution, says Webster's, is a "sudden, radical, or complete change . . . a basic reorientation." To anyone in the world of business, that sounds about right. We all sense that the changes surrounding us are not mere trends but the workings of large, unruly forces: the globalization of markets; the spread of information technology and computer networks; the dismantling of hierarchy, the structure that has essentially organized work since the mid-19th century. Growing up around these is a new, information-age economy, whose fundamental sources of wealth are knowledge and communication rather than natural resources and physical labor.
> Each of these transformations is a no fooling business revolution. Yet all are happening at the same time—and fast. They cause one another and affect one another. As they feed on one another, they nourish a feeling that business and society are in the midst of a revolution comparable in scale and consequence to the Industrial Revolution. (p. 66)

Much of what Stewart describes is apropos of the nonprofit world as well, but, in our view, to a less dramatic extent. For example, it is indeed true that the nonprofit sector faces rapid changes in technology. Nevertheless, the degree to which programs and services are impacting the nonprofit sector is not universal. For example, an orchestra still requires the presence of live musicians on stage in white tie and tails. Most likely, as this live concert is in full swing, camera technicians are taping the performance for use on television, radio, CD-ROM, and so on. However, the musicians themselves will not be replaced by a series of black boxes playing Mozart.

The same is true in post–secondary education. Although distance learning is big business and is making an impact on the traditional delivery of pedagogy in the classroom, there will, in all likelihood, always be the classroom and the seminar room where students and teachers engage in real face-to-face time. Once again, automation will not uniformly or consistently obliterate or obviate the necessity of some form of personal interaction.

This ongoing dependence on the human touch directly contrasts with manufacturing firms that have become increasingly dependent on robotics and other forms of advanced technology to do their assembly work. This represents a radical and rapid change. The technology used to record a concert and distance learning are radical departures from the past but are not truly rapid or breakthrough in the purist definition of reengineering.

In many ways, therefore, reengineering in the nonprofit has more of an incremental rather than a breakthrough feel, although what may appear to be incremental from the corporate perspective may, indeed, be breakthrough for the nonprofit. This is in large measure due to the "we have always done it that way" mentality of the nonprofit. As there is no profit and loss statement per se, productivity gains or enhancements are typically viewed incrementally. An example from the world of higher education reinforces this point.

CASE STUDY

Renaissance Women: The People Who Make the System Work

For over a century, the faculty of the University of Chicago has been supported by a traditional academic infrastructure. In descending order of authority, the members of the faculty are served and concurrently guided by the Office of the Provost, their particular dean's office, their department head, and their departmental secretary or assistant.

Clearly, the most important relationship in this hierarchy is the one a faculty member has with his/her departmental secretary/ assistant. Most typically, this "Renaissance woman" has an institutional memory, which is the envy of senior administrators. She knows through experience and intuition where the budget dollars reside, who will get the employee action form through the Human Resources Office, and what sponsored grants accountant will get her the most up-to-date read of her faculty members' research budget that has to be submitted to the NIH by the end of the month.

Recently, the university received the reengineering report of a consulting firm that suggested the abolition of the traditional faculty/secretary relationship and the creation of "local transaction centers" to serve clusters of departments and/or faculty to prevent costly duplication and fragmentation of effort at the departmental level.

This new paradigm, which is slated to save millions of dollars in administrative processes, calls for the creation of a cadre of professional and support staff that would provide individual faculty members with a center for human resources, accounting, procurement, financial reporting, and related administrative activities. The savings generated would be reallocated to support academic programs.

This is a radical redesign for higher education, but the university's culture will mitigate its rapid or immediate implementation. The concept is currently being reviewed by a faculty/staff committee. It is the university's hope to enlist one of the deans as sponsor for a test site. In all likelihood, it will take six to nine months to create and implement a test site.

In many nonprofit settings, executive directors and board members are sensitive to the use of the word *reengineering*, because it is associated with corporate downsizing and blood letting. Consequently, many are opting to talk of *redesign, transformation,* or *restructuring.* Many believe these terms speak more appropriately to the culture of their organizations and addresses more clearly the intended outcomes, as they sound less invasive or dramatic. Given this reality of the nonprofit culture, we present next the overall framework for reengineering or redesign.

THE FRAMEWORK FOR NONPROFIT REDESIGN/REENGINEERING

Reengineering is an iterative rather than a linear process. In this sense, it is much like strategic planning and resource allocation. Consequently, it is both a science and an art. Based on our experience, the framework outlined in Exhibit 3–4 provides the flexibility you and your colleagues will require to reengineer your organization. You will need to tailor these generic phases to fit the particular needs and culture of your organization. Answering these questions will help lay the foundation for

Phase	Key Question
1. Affirm/Revise/Mission/Vision	Do we have an up-to-date strategic plan? Can the plan, the mission, and the attendant vision guide the redesign? If not, what will it take to get started?
2. Reality Check	Do we have the will to undertake reengineering? Do we have change sponsors? How will we drive change in the organization?
3. Scope and Target	Will this be an organization-wide redesign or will we focus on key processes?
4. Redesign Targeted Processes	How can we redesign current processes to support our constituents more effectively and efficiently?
5. Assess Impact on Infrastructure	What impact will redesign have on people, technology, physical environment, policies, and regulation?
6. Implement	Who will be responsible for implementation? What is the time line? What are the tangible outcomes, and how do we measure them?
7. Assess Best Practices	Are we meeting our internally designed performance measures? Are we rewarding our employees, volunteers, and teams appropriately?

Exhibit 3–4   Reengineering Framework
Source: Pappas Consulting Group Inc., ©

your nonprofit's senior staff, the board, and the various work groups and teams assigned the responsibility to reengineer to get the process started. Exhibit 3–5 portrays these phases and their relationship to one another graphically.

The Pappas Group defines *process* in the context of reengineering or redesign as "a group of sequential, logically related activities that provides programs/services/learning to both internal and external constituents utilizing organizational resources (people, facilities, equipment, finances)."

METHODOLOGY FUNDAMENTALS

As is the case with strategic planning, leadership for reengineering needs to emanate from the highest levels of the organization, most notably with the executive director and the board of directors. Dr. Gwendolyn Calvert Baker, former national executive director of the YWCA of the USA, describes how her reengineering efforts, *Project Redesign*, were launched (*Redesigning the Nonprofit Organization*, Washington, DC: National Center for Nonprofit Boards, 1993, p. 4):

> In the fall of 1991, the board of directors and the board of trustees had also been thinking about change, and after one of their meetings, three of the trustees met with me to discuss the situation. That informal meeting was the catalyst for *Project Redesign*. Among those providing support for action were the board president and two trustees who were also former directors. With the signal from these leaders to move ahead, I knew that other support would be forthcoming, so we began to plan.

We have found that those nonprofits that have undertaken reengineering were most successful when they created a steering committee comprised of the best and brightest. Ideally, the membership should include staff and volunteers alike. In some cases, we have worked successfully with clients who have had a steering committee comprised of staff members as well as an advisory committee comprised of volunteers from across the organization (i.e., local, regional, and national) and the board. In such a scenario, the steering committee assumed day-to-day responsibility for the redesign itself, whereas the advisory committee was charged with critiquing project milestones and providing technical as well as qualitative input.

The steering committee should be charged initially with undertaking the first three phases of redesign. As the committee deliberates, it must

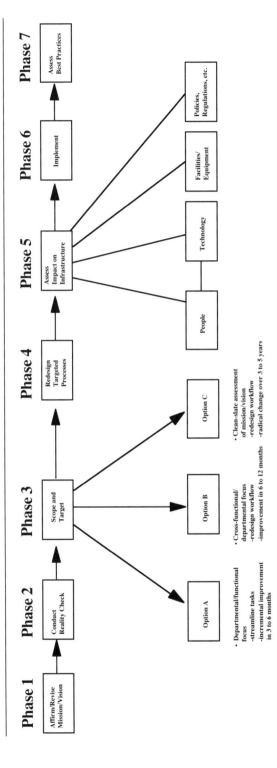

Exhibit 3–5 Graphic Representation of Reengineering Framework

develop an overall reengineering plan. Critical components of that plan are a time line, clearly defined objectives and scope, and a human resources plan. The latter is particularly crucial because undertakings such as these require significant changes in the volunteer and staff workforce. Such changes can include reallocation of personnel, elimination of positions, realignment of reporting relationships, the need for a new classification and pay plan, the need for training and development programs, and the like.

In addition, the steering committee should be forthright about why reengineering is being undertaken. The committee must be explicit about the objectives: Are they cost-cutting, improved service levels, or a balance of both? It also needs to be explicit about how cost savings will be applied. For example, will the cost savings be applied to investments in technology, facilities, equipment, training, staff development, or the provision of core services (education, programs, and services)?

Finally, the committee must determine whether it has the expertise to conduct such a project on its own or whether it requires the input, technical expertise, or facilitation assistance of a consultant.

Phase 4, Redesign of Targeted Processes, requires a disciplined approach. This two-tier phase first asks users and initiators of processes to assess existing program and service delivery mechanisms and process flows. It then turns to those same users and process/program initiators to create alternatives that are more streamlined and user friendly. This analysis requires one-on-one interviews with constituents, users, and staff as well as constituent/user focus groups and work groups. The objective of the interviews is to ascertain the current perception of the mission of the organization and its various operating entities, the organization structure, the degree to which technology is utilized, administrative bottlenecks, the degree to which policies and regulations (both internal and external to the organization) impact day-to-day operations, and so on.

The focus groups should be comprised of volunteers, users of services and programs, external constituents, and those who are initiators and/or participants in various administrative processes. We have found that it is particularly useful to segment participation among similar cohorts and to provide each participant at the close of the focus group with an evaluation instrument that ranks the perceived quality of service/program/administrative process delivery. For example, in the case of a national membership organization, arrange a series of group interviews for all local executive directors, local board/advisory committee members, national board members, national staff, and users of the services/programs.

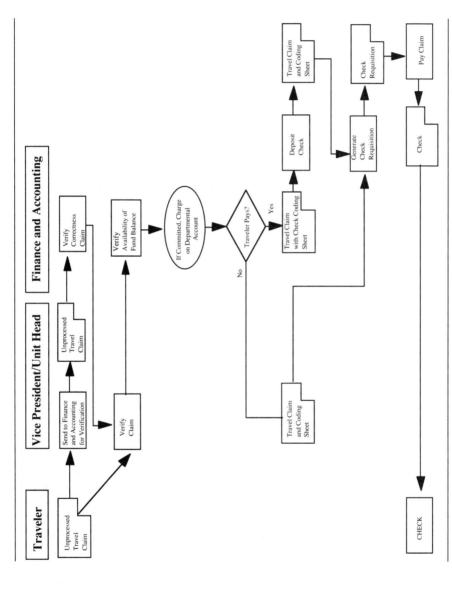

Exhibit 3–6 XYZ Nonprofit Travel Reimbursement

Perhaps the most technical aspect of Phase 4 is the flowcharting and redesign of administrative processes. The flowchart in Exhibit 3–6 provides a sense as to the level of detail that is required for a fundamental understanding of the process and subsequent redesign.

On the surface, these worksteps may appear labor intensive and, indeed, they are. However, do not forget that 80% of your organization's operating budget is comprised of salaries and those salaries translate into the people who touch every activity or transaction that is involved in a process.

We have found that the flowcharting can be done in one of two ways. It can be done by (1) members of your organization's finance department or by the internal auditor or (2) a group of approximately 8 to 12 users and process initiators collectively engaged in the flowcharting.

Typically, such work groups start off at a rather high functional level. Such discussions focus first on the general activities or steps of the process and require several sessions to complete the task. This is our preferred method of flowcharting as it engages staff (and volunteers where appropriate) in learning. It is not at all unusual, for example, to hear the following claims:

- "I didn't know you did it that way—we've always done it this way."
- "The accounts payable office is always sending back my travel reimbursement voucher, even though it was prepared by my supervisor's boss."
- "I don't understand why it takes so long to get my boss reimbursed for her travel."
- "Why does it take a parent so long to enroll her daughter in our child care program?"

Once the work group has flowcharted the process, the same work group should be charged with redesigning or reengineering the process in such a way as to eliminate unnecessary sign-offs and valueless steps. This is a time when the dynamics of the group gel and the creative juices flow. It is also a time when users and staff can begin to feel threatened as change is introduced and the potential for significant savings is realized.

In fact, during the course of consulting with nonprofits, the Pappas Consulting Group and KPMG Peat Marwick LLP developed a concept that addresses where significant costs are generated in an organization. This concept of *complex leverage* asserts that the greatest savings are

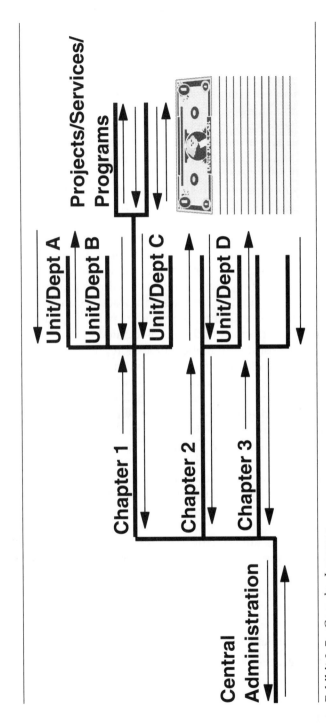

Exhibit 3–7 Complex Leverage

achieved in processes performed in the greatest number of places. In most nonprofit organizations, this includes processes in human resource management, financial accounting and reporting, procurement (purchasing and payables), contracts and grants administration, and travel reimbursement to name just a few.

Exhibit 3–7 graphically depicts a four-level sign-off and approval process. First the central administration initiates the process. The chapters receive the request from the central administration, and in turn the unit and projects with direct responsibility for the process get involved. The end user then responds and the process flows back up through the system. The stack of dollar bills in the exhibit underscores the expense of such multiple sign-offs.

You may decide that Phase 4 requires an even more in-depth appraisal using cost determination models. Such an approach may be particularly apropos in a complex national nonprofit organization or in a comprehensive university where there are multiple programs, services, and operating units. Once the activities and processes are identified, surveying administrators and service providers will help determine the kinds of activities performed and their associated costs.

Typically, such cost determination models report staff effort expended on task. Subsequently, they require individual staff to account for the amount of time (as a percentage) they spend on all the activities and functions they perform during the course of a year. Base salary and benefits are reported and the costs associated with a particular staff member's efforts can be compared with others in the organization.

In addition to understanding how staff spend their time, fragmentation and duplication of activity across the nonprofit can be determined. Exhibit 3–8 contains an example of an activity description for the human resources function of a large national nonprofit organization. The reports generated by such a program would indicate individual effort on task as well as the costs in aggregate of the human resources function, for example. Since the reports are structured by organizational unit, you will be able to determine the degree of fragmentation and duplication and the associated costs.

Upon completion of all of the tasks enumerated for Phase 4, the organization will have

- Defined its fundamental administrative and programmatic processes.
- Identified targets for redesign and begun the process of redesign/ reengineering.
- Established priorities for action.
- Estimated cost savings.

Activity Name	Activity Description
Complete human resource forms	Complete the following forms: • Request for recruitment • Personnel action form (PAF) • Personal data form (PDF) • Other personnel and payroll forms
Review compensation and classification requests	Review requests for compensation and classification of new and existing positions.
Design, develop, and maintain applicant tracking system	Design, develop, and maintain programs for applicant tracking system. Specify, develop, and produce reports for compensation and classification requests.
Update employee records	Complete, route, or approve Performance Action forms for continuing appointments and updates such as address changes or pay rate changes; enter and file official record of all employee data and actions. Enter employee benefits data. Copy, input, file, or otherwise maintain employee records in a manual or automated information system maintained by the unit. Include time spent reconciling unit data to central office records.
Design, develop, and maintain employee records system	Design, develop, and maintain programs for unit or employee records systems, database, or spreadsheet. Specify, develop, and produce reports for the above.
Provide formal orientation and training to employees	Prepare for and provide formal training to employees; attend training sessions provided by Human Resources.
Provide benefits counseling; counsel employees	Assist employees in understanding benefits available; provide assistance in completing paperwork for benefits election. Provide counseling to employees related to career, performance, other issues.
Process time reporting	Gather, process, approve, submit, and/or enter employee time for payroll processing.
Process payrolls	Verification, balancing, reporting, funding, and the like associated with payroll processing.

Activity Name	Activity Description
Sort, distribute payroll checks	Sort, distribute payroll checks.
Perform post-payroll processing	Produce reports; forward benefits payments and reports to benefit providers, and the like; other post-payroll processing activities.
Perform W-2 processing	Review W-2 data; adjust records; print and distribute W-2s.
Evaluate employee performance	Develop personnel evaluations; provide support to supervisors in using the form/procedures; conduct evaluations.
Support effort reporting	Distribute, track, collect, transport, and/or file effort reports.
Establish and interpret human resources policy and procedure; recruit and evaluate candidates for employment; perform employee relations activities; manage benefit plans	Set organization-wide human resources guidelines, policies, and procedures; provide information; implement procedures; develop and maintain documentation. Identify need for new position or reclassification; prepare job description. Recruit and evaluate employees. Perform employee relations activities including those related to grievances and disciplinary matters. Create, negotiate, administer benefit plans.
Other management of human resources process	Activities related to managing the human resources process that may not be listed above or do not individually total 5% of effort.
Other support of human resources process	Activities in support of the human resources process which may not be listed above or do not individually total 5% of effort.

Exhibit 3–8   Activity Description: The Human Resource Function

In many ways, the work of Phase 4 is rather clinical. Phase 5, on the other hand, is where the proverbial rubber hits the road. The organization now needs to assess the impact of redesigned/reengineered processes on people, technology, facilities and equipment, policies, regulations, and so on.

The people part of Phase 5 is among the most difficult to manage. It is at this juncture that your organization must make decisions about people's lives: Who has the skills, disposition, and commitment to assume additional responsibility? Who has the capacity to thrive in an environment of continuous change? Who is incapable of or unwilling to change? How can people be redeployed to newly created positions and what kinds of investments in training and development need to be made? How do we work with the unions to complete our reduction in force? What is the impact on our classification and pay plan as we make changes to our program and service delivery mechanisms and administrative process flows?

Typically, technology will emerge as an area requiring substantial investment. In all likelihood, you will find that your nonprofit requires technology that allows the initiator or front-end user of a process on-line access. This means the creation of a strategic systems plan if one does not already exist in your organization and subsequent decisions about hardware, software, networks, and telecommunications. It will also invariably require that you assess the capacity of staff and volunteers alike to function with the new technology. This, in turn, necessitates the development of a training program.

As you assess the impact of redesigned processes on your nonprofit's infrastructure in Phase 5, you will also need to determine the impact on facilities and equipment. If, for example, one of the YMCA's goals is to provide touch-tone telephone registration for karate and swimming classes, an analysis of costs needs to be undertaken for the provision of such technology and support staff. Or, if you are anxious to create a people-friendly service environment in which a museum visitor goes to one center to have her questions answered about gallery locations, the location of the lecture on ancient Egypt and the pharaohs, as well as the operating hours of the retail store and cafeteria, such a customer-service center might require the reallocation of office space and the construction of a new facility.

Finally, the fourth component, policies and regulations, must be addressed. For example, what impact does the redesign of targeted processes have on the nonprofit's policies concerning human resource management? How will volunteers be utilized in the new paradigm? If your organization is bound by certain federal or state regulations and your streamlining of the staff hiring process flies in the face of state requirements, how do you go about working with similar organizations to instigate change at the state level? With whom should you meet at that level? Which state-run departments are likely to be responsible for the process? What will motivate or drive them to change? Once again, we refer to the National office of the YWCA of the USA as they have chronicled these organizational redesign and have made it available through the auspices of the Center for Nonprofit Governing Boards.

CASE STUDY

Project Redesign: The Human Impact

The new structure of the national office of the YWCA of the USA required a 50% reduction in staff. As a result, on July 31, 1992, six months after the introduction of Project Redesign, the entire staff of the YWCA of the USA was asked to resign. Those who wished to remain with the national office were asked to reapply.

The requirements for dismissing union staff were applied to all terminations, including notice provisions of up to four months. Within sixty days, terminations had been processed, job descriptions for the new positions written and posted, and the rehiring process had begun.

This action had a number of purposes. Job terminations are never easy and are the the most difficult part of the project. Three actions were critical to this process. First, the initial announcement about Project Redesign informed staff that no one could be promised a position in the new organization; thus, all staff might lose their jobs. Second, a generous early retirement program eased the termination process. Therefore, a career transition firm was on site on the day of termination announcements. The firm provided counseling and conducted a variety of workshops to help the staff with interviewing techniques, resume writing, and other skills needed to seek new positions.

The next step was the phasing out of activities and functions that no longer fit the new design and gearing up for new functions and activities in preparation for the final stage of the process—transition.

Phase 6 requires the development of a clearly articulated implementation plan. Among the elements of such a plan are

- Detailed recommendations
- Dates for implementing individual recommendations
- Designation of the persons responsible for implementation
- Estimates of the financial implications of individual recommendations
  - technology
  - facilities/equipment

- training/development
- policies, procedures, regulations
- Proposed tables of organization and staffing levels
- Redesigned work flows and dates for implantation
- Work plans for senior staff to monitor progress and report to the board
- Change management issues that might provide obstacles to implementation (see Chapter 9 for details)

We recommend that such an implementation plan be developed by the senior leadership team of your organization with input from those staff and volunteers who helped redesign program and service delivery elements and administrative processes and assessed the impact of such change on the people, technology, facilities, equipment, and policies/regulations of your nonprofit.

In our view, a summary of such an implementation plan should be presented to board members to give them a clear and tangible understanding of the degree to which change will be necessary at both the volunteer and staff levels. Such a plan should also give them an assessment of the impact (both positive and negative) on service and program delivery to your organization's constituents.

Phase 7, Assess Best Practices, requires that a measurement and accountability system be established. In the nonprofit sector, where measurement is particularly difficult to define and obtain, such best practices assessments can range from an informal, manual collection of information and an ad hoc analysis system to a more sophisticated one. We have found, however, that the level of measurement sophistication is often related to the criticality and visibility of the particular process to the mission and external constituents. Such processes include but are not limited to program delivery, service delivery, administrative processes, and degree to which learning occurs in a class, lab, or in the field. Issues related to establishing and implementing performance measures for the nonprofit are the subject of Chapter 8.

FIRSTHAND EXPERIENCES

Before we provide some firsthand reengineering experiences from the world of the nonprofit, let us recall what reengineering is:

- A cross functional/organizational initiative
- Process (service, program, learning, administration) focused

- Simultaneous change to organizational design, culture, technology, facilities, and equipment
- Designed to enable radical/fundamental performance improvements

Here are what your colleagues tell us about successful reengineering:

- Allow sufficient time for your redesign process to achieve your goals but do not prolong the process.
- Allow sufficient time for organizational transition/transformation.
- Be sanguine about the implications of change that will occur as the result of restructuring and reengineering.
- Ensure that the project is mission based and constituency driven.
- Give time and thought to creating a vision.
- Organize an approach that reflects the needs, culture, and existing organizational/governance aspects of your organization.
- Develop a plan that is cross-functional, inclusive, and interactive and that will not render your current organization dysfunctional.
- Solicit support for the project from all internal and external constituents.
- Develop and clearly communicate a set of guidelines for the process.
- Make sure project leaders are the best, brightest, and most respected in your organization and that they are committed to its mission.
- Challenge everything. Conventional wisdom may not always apply.
- Manage change before, during, and after the project.
- Involve human resources and information technology experts throughout.
- Select a project team with industry and functional experience. Determine whether consultants should be utilized.

We would be remiss if we did not indicate to you where we, in our capacity as consultants, have seen restructuring/reengineering efforts flounder or fail or not be as successful as they had the potential to be. The following situations and circumstances hindered success:

- Politics were more important than organizational mission.
- Individual as opposed to organization-wide agendas were priorities.

- Executive directors under fire believed that undertaking a reengineering project would deflect the animus of a less-than-supportive board in other directions.
- The executive director left in the early stages of transition and had not invested sponsorship throughout the senior management team.
- Staff throughout the organization had not learned to say "no" to those constituents out in the field or out in the academic departments.
- Major processes that cut across the entire organization remained unexamined.
- Staff were not appropriately trained and developed to cope with increased technology and a flattened, front-end driven organization.
- Outsourcing/privatizing were viewed as ways to circumvent dealing with fundamental personnel and management deficiencies. (that is, hiring a private firm to deliver the support services—plant maintenance, custodial services, bookstore, foodservice, computing—that the nonprofit organization would normally provide with its own staff.)
- The board did not understand fully the significance and ramifications of the change effort.
- The compensation, performance appraisal, and resource allocation processes were not redesigned to support the newly constituted organization and culture.

CHAPTER FOUR

The Vocation of Voluntarism

One of the unique attributes of the nonprofit sector is the volunteer. Volunteers serve in many capacities: They read to those who are illiterate, help out hospice patients and their families, coach little league teams, sell greeting cards, serve as docents, and perform many other functions.

At this level, the contributed services of these volunteers support the day-to-day operations, programs, and services of the nonprofit. At the organization-wide level, volunteers serve as board members, most commonly without remuneration, and are charged with the legal and fiduciary well-being of the entities they serve.

Tremendous changes are currently at play that will greatly influence the traditional manner in which the nonprofit sector has gone about attracting and retaining volunteers at both the operating and board levels. First, there are shifting patterns of voluntarism and dramatic changes in the demographics of the American population. Overall, the American population is aging and becoming more racially and ethnically diverse. The majority of women work, reducing considerably the time available to this cohort for volunteer activities. Workplace stress and concerns about job security lead employees to dedicate 100% of their efforts to their paid jobs.

A second factor involves issues external to the world of the nonprofit itself. Nancy R. Axelrod, president of the National Center for Nonprofit Boards, states in the September/October 1994 issue of *Board Member* (Vol. 3, No. 5, p. 3):

> At no time in our nation's history has such intense public scrutiny been focused on America's nonprofit organizations. The media, potential governmental regulators, scholars and the public are all questioning the role of nonprofits, the value of the sector's contributions to the common good, and the way individual organizations conduct their affairs.

In this new climate of scrutiny and accountability, the millions of individuals who serve on nonprofit boards have a critical role to play in strengthening the sector as a whole and in shaping its future.

Now more than ever, it's critical that board members consider the forest. Changes in the larger environment of the nonprofit sector also threaten individual nonprofits. Events that may seem unrelated to your organization—newspaper headlines in a distant city, a tax dispute in a state capital, or hearings in Washington—could, in fact, jeopardize your nonprofit's ability to carry out its mission.

This chapter provides an overview of changing volunteer patterns and what the sector must do to respond if it is to be successful in redesigning the manner in which it addresses its volunteers. Chapter 5, The Duty of Stewardship, addresses the vulnerability of current nonprofit boards and provides some suggested remedies in the form of a new paradigm for governance.

THE CHANGING VOLUNTEER PROFILE

People volunteer for many reasons: for example, a desire to help the needy, deep-seated religious convictions, or the need/desire to gain work experience.

In his 1988 treatise, *Based on the Nonprofit Economy* (Boston: Harvard University Press, 1980), Burton A. Weisbrod states that both economic theory and recent statistical research suggest that the amount of labor that people are willing to donate depends partly on economic forces, including tax laws and the available governmental programs that substitute for, or are complementary to, nonprofit sector programs and activities. For example, policies on taxes and public expenditures affect an individual's perceptions of the cost/benefit ratio inured to her/him as the result of volunteering. As Weisbrod points out: "The amount of donated time is influenced by the same governmental policies that influence private donations of money, but the effects of the changes in governmental activity on the supply of volunteer labor are more complex because the goals of the people who supply labor are more varied than are those of people who donate money" (p. 134).

Individuals who volunteer to gain work experience are not likely to increase their hours of contributed services merely because the government has cut back on social services spending. Indeed, it is likely that same individual will reduce her/his level of unpaid commitment or withdraw as a volunteer in lieu of a paying job.

A Gallup survey of volunteers for the period 1981–1985, as cited by Weisbrod (1988, p. 134), indicates that

- The stated reason for volunteers "to learn and get experience" or to help "get a job" (i.e., preparing for entry into the labor market) dropped slightly from 11% to 10%.

- Seventeen percent of volunteers under age 35 reported providing charitable services for the purpose of "getting a job," whereas only 5% of volunteers age 35 to 64 stated so, and no one age 65 or over gave that reason. Such results should not be surprising as investment in learning and experience should inure greater long-term benefits for younger people who anticipate decades of work life.

- Forty-five percent of volunteers in 1981 and 52% of volunteers in 1985 reported that their motivation for volunteering was "to do something useful to help others." Of those reporting such helping motivations, there was little variation among age groups, with the exception of the 25 to 34-year-old cohort, in which 45% articulated such a motivation.

- The tax rate on money income affects the supply of unpaid labor. Reduced income tax rates, by increasing the after-tax income from work, have a "substitution effect," shifting incentives in favor of money-making activities and away from volunteering and donating money.

Since this 1981–1985 Gallup poll was conducted, some significant changes have occurred in the nation's overall economy. For example, the economy was hit by two major recessions in July 1990 and March 1991, and economic recovery has been slow and uneven across the country to this day. Employment uncertainty, national social problems, and dramatic changes in public policy are all converging to impact negatively the charitable behavior of individuals and corporations.

To study the impact of such volatile issues on the nonprofit, the Independent Sector, a Washington DC-based nonprofit organization serving the needs of the nonprofit sector, engaged the Gallup Organization to conduct in-home personal interviews with 1,509 adults 18 years of age and older during the period April 22 to May 15, 1994. These randomly selected interviewees were asked a series of questions about annual giving for their particular household as well as questions concerning their own voluntarism, motivations for giving and volunteering, and opinions and attitudes about charitable organizations.

The highlights of this 1994 Gallup poll included the following:

The Bad News

- An estimate that 89.2 million adults volunteered in 1993 represents a 5% decline from the 94.2 million who volunteered in 1991.

- In 1993, adults 18 years of age or older volunteered an average of two hours per week. (In 1993 there were 187.1 million adults 18 years or older.) In 1991, 184.4 million adults volunteered 2.1 hours per week. The average hours volunteered per week in 1993 for all adults 18 years of age or older, including nonvolunteers, was 2.0. There were 187.1 million adults 18 years of age or older. These findings are similar to the average of 2.1 hours volunteered per week among 184.4 million adults in 1991.

- Forty-eight percent of respondents reported that they volunteered in 1993, representing a decline from 51% who reported volunteering in 1991 and the 54% in 1989 according to figures cited in The Independent Sector's *Giving and Volunteering*, Volume I (1994). Most of the decline in volunteering came in the form of "informal volunteering." Such informal volunteering involves helping neighbors or organizations on an ad hoc basis by baby-sitting or baking cookies for a school fair as opposed to "formal" volunteering that involves regular work for an organization, such as candy striping, tutoring, data entry, selling greeting cards, and reading to the infirm. The percentage of respondents that reported volunteering on an informal basis declined from 23% in 1991 to 17% in 1993.

- Volunteers gave an estimated total of 19.5 billion hours in both formal and informal volunteering in 1993, about 5% lower than the total of 20.5 billion hours in 1991. Americans who volunteered formally in 1993 gave 15.0 billion hours, representing less than a 2% decrease from the 15.2 billion hours they gave in 1991. These hours represent the equivalent of 8.8 million full-time employees in 1993, compared with 9.0 million equivalent full-time employees in 1991. The value of volunteer time was estimated at $182 billion in 1993, compared with $176 billion in 1991. Americans who volunteered informally gave 4.5 billion hours in 1993, which represents a 15% decrease from the 5.3 billion hours given in 1991.

- More than one out of four of all volunteers (27%) volunteered five hours per week or more in 1993, which was about the same percentage as in 1991. Based on these findings, it is estimated that 23.6 million adults volunteered five or more hours per week in 1993, which is 6% below the 25.2 million who did so in 1991.

- Volunteering has a direct relationship to the amount of contributions—that is, more volunteer time means more money donated.

- Males, African Americans, people of Hispanic origin, people between the ages of 25 and 44, respondents with household income ranges of $40,000 to $50,000 and $75,000 and above, Catholics, single persons, persons employed full time, and respondents with some college or college graduates reported a 5% decline in the rate of volunteering.

The Good News

- Only two demographic groups showed an increase of 5% or more in their rate of volunteering from 1991 to 1993—those respondents age 75 years or older and retired people.

In short, this latest Gallup survey indicates that when economic instability affects a substantial proportion of the population, those who contribute give less and to fewer organizations. Although nearly half of the nation's population continues to volunteer, a gradual decline in volunteering from 54% in 1989 to 48% in 1993 has occurred. In addition to a significant decline in the average number of hours per week volunteered, volunteers have reported a decline of 10% in the number of assignments. These trends demand a fresh look at reengineering the role and responsibility of the volunteer.

THE TIP OF THE DEMOGRAPHIC AND LEGISLATIVE ICEBERG

The trends we have just enumerated are troublesome. However, these trends are simply the tip of the iceberg. The degree to which voluntarism and the nonprofit sector will be challenged is great. For example, did you know that

- The greatest increase in the number of nonprofits occurred for those that address the environment; animal-related issues; medical research; crime and legal issues; food, agriculture, and nutrition; human services; international causes; community improvement; social sciences; and religion. As a consequence, resources are not being funnelled into any particular segment.
- In 1992, the American Association of Fund Raising Counsel reported that donations to nonprofit organizations rose to $123.4 billion from 1991, an increase of 6.4%. The major source of donations was people age 45 to 54, and many observers are afraid that as the baby

boom generation ages, it will not be as generous as preceding generations because of differences in values that do not hold dear philanthropic giving.

- The percentage of membership dues associated with lobbying by trade and social organizations [Sections 501 (c)(4)s] that has often been deductible as a business expense is currently being challenged by the IRS. This will have a negative effect on membership drives in the future.

- The 1993 federal tax regulations, which require nonprofits to provide receipts to contributors of $250 or more and give those donors specific information about the deductibility of their gifts, have generated yet another administrative reporting burden for nonprofit organizations.

- A number of states and many local communities (Evanston, Illinois, and Buffalo, New York, for example) are challenging the property tax exemption of nonprofit organizations, because these nonprofit entities utilize municipal services without directly paying for them.

- Small businesses continue to join forces to challenge the tax-exempt status of the nonprofit sector in the delivery of for-profit activities even though revenue-generating or auxiliary service operations support the mission of the nonprofit.

- The House Republicans' "Contract with America," which proposes significant welfare system overhaul, has the potential to shift the programmatic and financial burden of supporting families and children to the nonprofit sector.

- Many nonprofit executive directors worry that the withdrawal of federal aid to arts groups, schools, social service organizations, environmental programs, and other groups currently proposed by the Republican-dominated House of Representatives will lead to a considerable loss of private giving because federal funding often motivates others to give.

- Even small reductions in federal spending will make it more difficult for nonprofit groups to provide services. Many fear that small, community-based programs are particularly likely to be unable to continue to provide services.

- Although the minority population continues to grow rapidly (according to the 1982 Workforce 2000 study and others), 20% to 40% of the prospective volunteer and employee pool this growth represents is being ignored.

What does this say about the future of the nonprofit sector in general and of voluntarism in particular? Simply put, both the sector as a whole and the millions of Americans who have traditionally supported the sector financially and philosophically and with contributed time/services are being buffeted by a host of converging demographic, financial, and social policy issues of incredible intensity. In some cruel irony, all of these factors are appearing at a time when the number of single-parent families is increasing, heads of households are most typically both working (be they traditional heterosexual relationships or lesbian or gay relationships), corporate America continues to downsize, and the stress level of families and individuals is becoming dysfunctional.

Most likely these personally and organizationally punishing trends will mean

- The number of volunteers and the number of hours of contributed services they provide the sector will continue to decrease.
- The recent downward spiral in individual and corporate giving will continue. (Because the number of hours a volunteer serves and the amount of the charitable donation he/she gives are directly related, this dynamic is particularly troublesome.)
- Younger volunteers who are attempting to gain employment will use the nonprofit primarily for their own benefit rather than for the benefit of the organization. Once they have secured a paying job, in all likelihood, they will not continue to contribute their time or money.
- A further, rapid decline in informal volunteering will occur as the multiple demands on heads of households and single parents increase.
- Persons of color will not be an influential force in or percentage of the volunteer marketplace.
- The number of volunteers age 75 or greater will cease to grow when the baby boomers, who have a distinct set of social values, reach that age.

These trends dictate that nonprofit executive directors and their boards begin to investigate ways in which to reengineer or redesign the volunteer component of their organization. The following section of this chapter describes the way in which your nonprofit can begin to understand more fully those who comprise the volunteer workforce and how these individuals can be persuaded to play a role (or an even greater role) in positioning your organization's cause.

CREATING A NEW VOLUNTEER PARADIGM

In Chapter 1, as well as in the previous sections of this chapter, we have talked about the significant financial impact of the nonprofit sector in general and of the contributed services volunteers provide these entities and the American economy as a whole. Ironically, there is a value/cost paradox of voluntarism, and we believe that this paradox must be better understood as we begin to create a new volunteer paradigm.

What do we mean by a value/cost paradox? The case study below, based on our vivid memory of staff-volunteer interaction at the Los Angeles office of the United States Committee for UNICEF, captures this contradiction perfectly.

CASE STUDY

The Value/Cost Paradox

I was in the Los Angeles Office of the United States Committee for UNICEF conducting a series of interviews with staff and leadership team members. I was into my second day of interviews and was quietly seated in the organization's only conference room. As is the case with most nonprofits I have worked with, the conference room served multiple purposes: It served as a storage room for UNICEF greeting cards and associated retail merchandise, as a storage room for paper and other supplies, as the board room, and as an office for the many volunteers of the greater Los Angeles area.

The conference room had glass walls on two sides and a door, which at the time was slightly ajar. I was seated at one end of the conference table sorting out my interview notes and was facing directly into one of the glass-enclosed offices across the hall. I heard the doorbell ring, and as I glanced up from my seat, I noticed one of the young women staff escort a diminutive octogenarian with all the lust of life that reminded me so hauntingly of my father, who had just passed away. The ever-so-gracious gentleman introduced himself to me and told me he was there to continue his assignment cleaning up the mailing list. He then described to me in detail why this assignment was so important to UNICEF's fund-raising efforts.

The volunteer enthusiastically sat at his desk, logged in, and set about his assignment. That lasted ten minutes. For that ten minutes and every ten minutes thereafter, he would call out to the staff member responsible for greeting card sales and the mailing lists to enlist her help with the program. Every time he called across the office, she dutifully and most patiently responded, getting up and out of her chair upon every occasion to help him address one problem after another.

This lasted for approximately three hours and at the end of the day there was an additional set of updates and corrections to the lengthy and critical mailing list—created free of charge. The volunteer cheerfully announced that he had done what he had set about to accomplish for the day and would see the staff tomorrow afternoon. The staff warmly greeted the satisfied volunteer "good night" and resumed their work.

Indeed, the contributed services of the UNICEF volunteer were and continue to be of considerable value to the L.A. office and the U.S. Committee. However, there is significant staff cost to this effort in terms of both the provision of direct time as well as the productivity/sales of greeting cards; the time that the staff member would have typically given to greeting card sales was diverted to an important but nonetheless support activity.

When this volunteer aura is multiplied throughout the organization, it is much akin to the theory of complex leverage we presented in Chapter 3, which demonstrated how the actions taken at one level were duplicated at different levels throughout the organization. That is why we call this phenomenon the *value/cost paradox* of voluntarism and why the new paradigm must cogently address the most effective and efficient way of working with volunteers on a day-to-day basis.

How do you deal with this all-too-imperfect human/interpersonal element? The answer is with great personal care but with an eye to improving, *not* diminishing, the productivity of the volunteer and the staff member. On the one hand, you need to be sensitive to the good will that comes with the volunteer's contributed services and verbalize your appreciation to the volunteer. On the other hand, your nonprofit needs to outline specifically when and how such volunteer time should be used.

We describe ways in which to address this most sensitive issue as well as others in the section of this chapter entitled "Getting to Work."

In addition, the nonprofit must understand the trend associated with the distribution of volunteers across the sector and the percentage of the population 18 years old and older who volunteer, as well as their particular demographics. See Exhibits 4–1 and 4–2.

If these conditions and trends are understood in the context of the manifold societal changes that are occurring, nonprofits can begin to cluster their volunteers and potential volunteers in such a way as to ensure organizational strength and financial security.

Getting to Work

Designing a new volunteer paradigm for your organization should begin with the creation of a joint volunteer-staff committee that is charged with first identifying and then categorizing or stratifying current volunteers as well as volunteer prospects. The committee should start by asking the following questions that put volunteers into the organizational context of the nonprofit:

- Our organization serves a wide range of people, both internal and external to the nonprofit. Who are they?
- How well our organization serves this diverse set of individuals and groups is directly proportionate to the degree of future success we will enjoy. Specifically, are we doing a good job supporting the volunteers we have?
- The future success of our organization is also dependent on a clear and concise articulation of our mission and vision to current as well as potential volunteers. Are we clear about our mission and vision and have we communicated those adequately to our current and prospective volunteers?

Once these context-setting questions are answered, the following questions, which focus on the volunteers and their needs and expectations should be raised:

- What do our volunteers currently receive for giving their time and financial resources to our organization?
- What should each volunteer expect to receive from our organization that he/she currently does not receive? How can this be achieved?
- What does our organization currently get from our volunteers—time, in-kind gifts, donations, referrals to prospective donors?
- What should our organization expect to get from our current as well as prospective volunteers? How do we achieve this?

Once this series of questions is answered, the committee should then be charged with differentiating its volunteers from its prospective volunteers. Most organizations think of volunteers in a homogeneous manner—as if volunteers are all cast from the same mold or have the same attributes, motivations, needs, and wants. Indeed, nothing could be fur-

Demographic characteristic	March 1990		March 1988	
	Previous 12 months	Previous month	Previous 12 months	Previous month
Total	54	43	45	39
Sex				
Male	52	41	44	37
Female	56	45	47	41
Race				
White and other	57	45	48	41
nonwhite	37	29	—	—
Black	38	29	28	24
Hispanic[a]	36	30	27	23
Age				
18–24	43	32	42	35
25–34	62	49	45	38
35–44	64	52	54	48
45–54	50	44	48	41
55–64	51	41	47	10
65+	41	30	36	30
65–74	47	30	40	33
75+	32	27	29	25
Income				
Under $10,000	30	22	23	20
$10,000–$19,999	42	32	40	34
$20,000–$29,999	56	44	50	43
$30,000–$39,999	64	48	51	43
$40,000–$49,999	67	57	44	38
$50,000–$74,999	63	50	57	52
$75,000–$99,999	62	52	50	43
$100,000+	74	58	62	53
Marital Status				
Married	59	47	50	43
Single	44	34	40	33
Divorced, separated, or widowed	47	37	34	29
Employment Status				
Employed	60	47	49	43
Full time	57	45	48	41
Part time	72	60	54	48
Not employed	45	34	38	33

Exhibit 4–1 Percentage of Population 18 Years Old and Older Volunteering in Previous Month and 12 Months by Selected Characteristics in 1987 and 1989

Sources: Virginia A. Hodgkinson, Murray S. Weitzman, and the Gallup Organization, Inc., *Giving and Volunteering in the United States,* 1990 Edition, Table 1.19, p. 44. (Copyright and published by *Independent Sector,* Washington DC, 1990); and Virginia A. Hodgkinson and Murray S. Weitzman, *Dimensions of the Independent Sector,* 3rd ed., 1989 (Copyright and published by *Independent Sector,* Washington, D.C., 1989).

— = Not available. This category was not included in the 1988 survey.

[a] Hispanics may be of any race.

Jobs	1994	1992	1990	1988
Aide/assistant to paid employees	3.3%	2.5%	7.6%	6.2%
Aide to clergy	4.1	2.1	7.1	4.0
Assisting the elderly, handicapped, social service recipients, or homeless (not as part of an organization or group)	4.8	6.0	7.3	7.7
Baby-sitting (not as part of an organization or group)	4.1	5.1	3.3	5.9
Choir member or director	2.1	2.5	2.3	2.0
Church usher	1.9	1.1	1.5	1.5
Deacon or deaconess	0.6	0.6	0.4	1.0
Parish visitor or missionary	1.1	0.7	3.1	0.9
Sunday school or Bible teacher	4.7	3.7	2.1	3.3
Driver	2.0	3.0	4.3	2.5
Fund-raising for local organization	4.8	—	—	5.3
Board member or trustee	1.3	1.7	1.6	2.3
Office work (e.g., answering telephone, clerical work, but not for religious organizations)	2.2	2.6	2.8	2.1
Office work for religious organizations	1.8	1.7	—	—
Organization officer (elected or appointed)	0.8	1.4	1.0	1.3
Committee member	2.7	4.9	3.6	4.9
Campaign worker or election day worker	0.8	0.4	0.5	1.6
Cleaning or janitorial work	1.0	2.5	2.2	1.3
Assistant at blood bank or blood donation station	0.4	0.3	0.4	1.2
Hospital volunteer or assistant at nursing home	1.8	0.8	0.9	2.4
Visiting nurse	0.1	0.1	0.1	0.4
Fire, rescue or first aid squad volunteer	0.6	0.2	0.4	0.7
Coach, director, or recreational volunteer	2.7	3.2	2.1	3.3
Librarian or aide in library	0.6	0.5	0.4	0.6
Teacher or tutor (not as aide to paid employee)	3.4	4.6	2.6	3.5
Youth group leader or aide	3.5	4.8	3.1	3.3
Community coordinator	1.1	0.9	0.6	1.2
Counselor (Big Brother/Big Sister, substance abuse prevention)	1.3	1.0	1.1	0.9
Social service counselor	0.9	0.8	0.8	0.6
Arts volunteer (theater, arts, and music)	1.1	1.6	1.5	1.6
Usher, guide, or tour leader	0.3	0.5	0.6	0.4

Jobs	1994	1992	1990	1988
Civic or social group spokesperson	0.8	1.3	1.3	1.1
Meeting or convention planner	1.8	2.2	1.1	1.7
Poll taker	0.1	0.0	0.2	0.4
Telephone hotline volunteer	0.7	0.6	—	—
Unpaid blood donor	1.0	0.4	—	—
Other religious volunteer work	6.0	4.3	—	—
Other	10.5	9.8	5.5	1.3
Don't know	17.2	19.6	26.6	32.7

Exhibit 4–2 Distribution of Volunteer Jobs in the Past Month (February–March 1988, 1990, 1992, and April–May 1994 in percentages of volunteers.)[a]
Sources: Virginia A. Hodgkinson, Murray S. Weitzman, and the Gallup Organization, Inc., *Giving and Volunteering in the United States,* 1990 Edition, p. 26. (Copyright and published by *Independent Sector,* Washington, D.C. 1990.)
[a]Data from the 39% of respondents in 1988, the 43% in 1990, the 39% in 1992, and the 39% in 1994 who volunteered in the last month.
—Not available. This category was not included in the survey for that year.

ther from the truth. Volunteers vary in what they expect from and what they are willing to give to an organization (refer to the stakeholder analysis described in Chapter 2). Therefore, you have to understand your volunteers before you can develop effective strategies to move them from where they are to where you want them to be in relationship to the organization. We recommend that you use one of the exercises contained in the *Constituency Development Manual* of the *Resource Development System* © that is geared to defining constituencies. We have tailored this constituency development assessment for volunteers in Exhibit 4–3.

The definition of the initial stratification of volunteers follows:

Mass Volunteers: These volunteers, drawn from the general public, include individuals who you believe might have an interest in your cause or the mission of your organization. At this level of voluntarism, your objective is to determine how to encourage the volunteer to become involved at an entry level. One approach is to develop targeted messages that tell potential volunteers about the organization through a public service announcement and then follow up with a personal call recruiting them to participate.

Select Volunteers: Volunteers who have demonstrated a sustained interest/participation in your organization through regular contributions or active involvement constitute the select category. Typically, these are

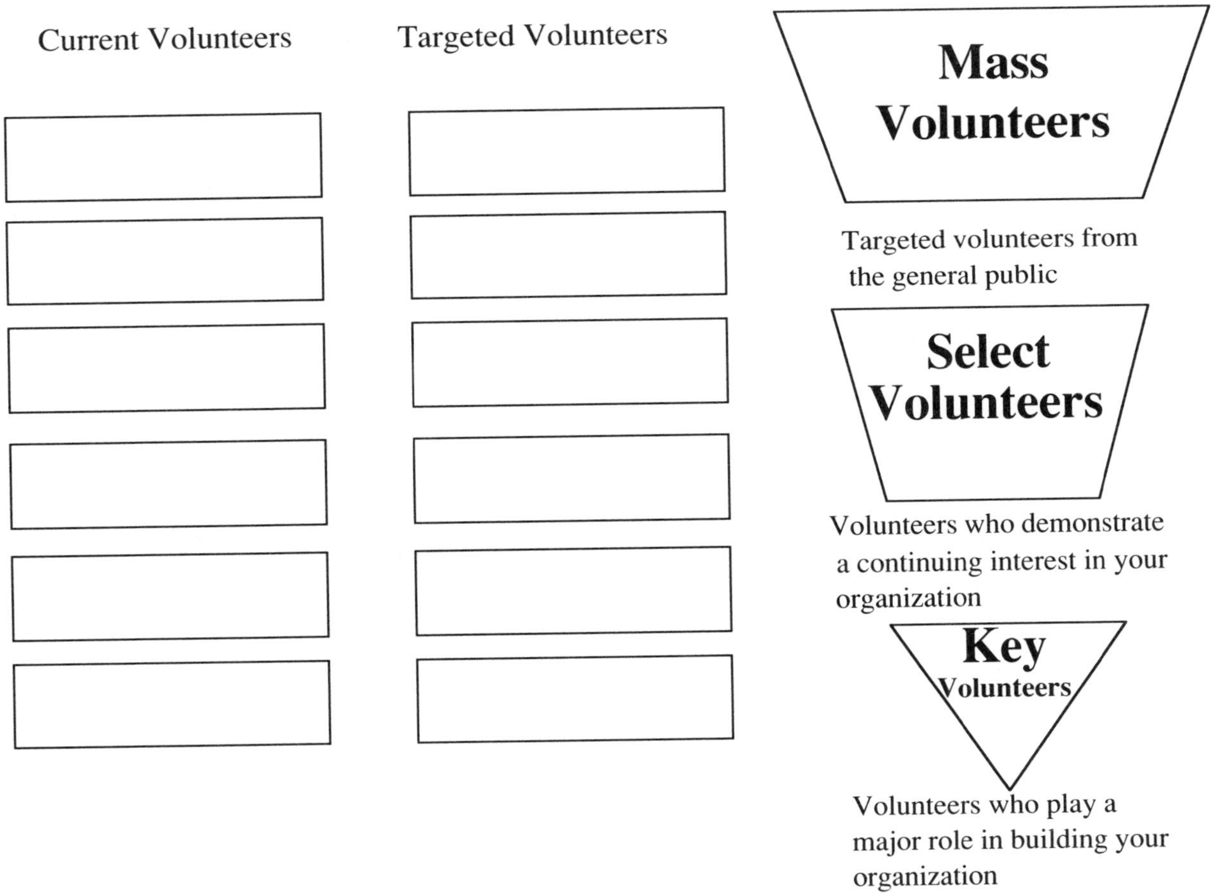

Mass Volunteers

Targeted volunteers from the general public

Select Volunteers

Volunteers who demonstrate a continuing interest in your organization

Key Volunteers

Volunteers who play a major role in building your organization

Current Volunteers

Targeted Volunteers

Exhibit 4-3 Volunteer Stratification Exercise

the individuals who staff your programs, auxiliaries, and special advisory/program boards and/or are among your significant donors.

Key Volunteers: These are the people who play a major and continuing role. Most typically, they include the board of directors and major donors. This category contains your most able and stalwart of leaders. This is the cohort that shapes the future of your organization in partnership with the senior staff.

Upon completion of this stratification exercise, we encourage you to take an even more in-depth view of the three stratified levels and collect and assess such demographic data as gender, age, race/ethnicity, average household income, level/potential of giving, work experience, specialized skill sets, and so on in order to target your recruitment efforts more effectively.

To reiterate, it is important that you take the time to understand your current and potential volunteer base, as it is an extraordinarily important asset. Without these individuals, many nonprofits could not function effectively or, for that matter, exist. As we pointed out earlier with our poignant example of the octogenarian in the Los Angeles office of the United States Committee for UNICEF, the value/cost paradox of the volunteer must be addressed head-on. Even though people may be willing to provide their time gratis, they are not automatically helpful. In short, volunteers, like staff, must be managed (see Chapter 6).

For those volunteers who participate in the direct provision of service/care/program delivery (e.g., a hospice volunteer, a candy striper, a docent, a tutor), their tasks/jobs are difficult to quantify. For those volunteers who are involved in the administrative support roles of the organization (e.g., stuffing envelopes, answering telephones, serving as secretarial backup), their work is clearly discernible and measurable.

In both cases, the volunteer must have a clearly defined role and must be managed and supported by the professional staff. In turn, volunteers must be supportive of the staff. The roles and responsibilities of the staff must be as carefully defined as those of the volunteer to avoid any possible misunderstanding or conflict among and between staff and volunteers. Further, it is absolutely essential that volunteers be told how their contributions of time and money will be used, and their input regarding how the money should be spent should be sought.

Some New Paradigms Emerge

Nonprofits across the country are just beginning to fully grasp the necessity of developing intentional strategies to recruit and retain volunteers throughout their organization—be it at the local or national level or both.

We provide three case studies. The first describes what Hadassah, the Women's Zionist Organization of America, is currently undertaking to combat the declining number of young volunteers in the organization. The second describes some of the interesting programs a few forward-thinking corporations are attempting to develop to attract families to the world of volunteering. The third highlights the rather unorthodox approach the founders of New York Cares adopted to recruit and retain the oft maligned "yuppies."

CASE STUDY

The Women Behind the Zionist Movement

Hadassah is one of the most venerable women's and Jewish organizations in the United States. Founded by Henrietta Szold in 1912, prior to the Balfour Declaration, Hadassah was and remains at the forefront of the world Zionist movement and was instrumental in the founding of the state of Israel. Hadassah is a service, educational, and philanthropic organization that has long supported path-breaking medical research and clinical care. Hadassah International exists on four continents. In the United States, Hadassah has 1,500 chapters and groups nationwide.

Marlene Post, president of Hadassah in 1995, articulated in a clear and powerful manner the challenge of the changing profile of voluntarism in women's organizations:

> As men have always been assumed to be the breadwinners in this country, the organizations they founded or which exclusively served the world of boys or men at their founding, were originally staffed with professionals as the men did not have the time to devote full-time to serve as *working* volunteers. The situation, however, was different for women's organizations. Most typically, women did not work outside the home as professional staff but were expected, in many social circles, to *work* as volunteers. As a result, there were no or very limited numbers of professional staff in these organizations founded by women. As a result, many of the men's organizations today are at a much more managerially sophisticated level because they have been managed professionally for a long time.

Indeed, the challenge for Hadassah is great. Volunteers have literally provided hands-on management of various programs and services since its founding. The heads of divisions and units have historically been volunteers who came to Hadassah House in New York City, sat at their desks, and directed the activities of other volunteers and a small cadre of secretarial and support staff for forty hours a week on average.

These dedicated women are beginning to retire at an exponential rate while their daughters and granddaughters are fully consumed with paid work, raising children, and finding convenient day care programs. These rapidly changing demographics have convinced the board to make a series of bold strategic decisions regarding the deployment of human resources—be they paid staff or volunteers.

Using an inclusive strategic planning process as its blueprint, Hadassah is incrementally building a professional staff infrastructure to support its new paradigm as a volunteer-led and staff-managed organization.

In our view, the challenge of such implementation from the human perspective is profound. Not only has Hadassah begun to lose its founding mothers, it has begun to lose an extraordinary legacy that cannot be replaced. Celebrating the contributions of these women and simultaneously redesigning the fundamental infrastructure of the organization will require will and compassion. This is radical redesign or reengineering for this nonprofit.

Another case in point is the "Family Matters Program" developed by the Points of Light Foundation.

CASE STUDY

The Family as Volunteer

In order to infuse the world of nonprofits with a cadre of young volunteers, the Points of Light Foundation has created the "Family Matters Program." This program was developed as the result of research that emanated from two studies that found that when Americans volunteered their time to nonprofits, they often did so with family members. A Points of Light–directed poll of 1,002 adults conducted by the George H. Gallup International Institute indicated that 36% of Americans currently volunteer with a family member and that 80% of these said they had done so for at least three years.

Virginia Austin, Family Matters program director, states: "Once it starts, volunteering is an activity that families will continue."

Austin further explains that the program is particularly important as it hopes to pass on the eleemosynary aspect of volunteering to younger generations.

In a survey conducted by the Conference Board, a business-research organization, 166 large corporations reported that they encouraged employees to include family members in company-sponsored volunteer projects. Such corporations, however, reported significant obstacles to such family-centered programs. Specifically, one quarter of the respondents said that it was difficult to find volunteer activities for families and 22% of the public affairs officers interviewed reported that corporate managers themselves were often not interested in promoting such family volunteer projects.

This case study provides insight into the challenges the non-profit and the corporate world alike face when introducing a new paradigm of volunteering—in this case, the volunteer as family.

CASE STUDY

Reaching Out to New Volunteers: New York Cares— 1986 and 1994

In the Winter 1989 issue of *Amherst*, that college's alumni magazine, Terry Y. Allen describes the founding of a New York–based nonprofit organization:

> In the mid-1980s, Noah Gotbaum was like many of his contemporaries, living in Manhattan and working an average of 12–14 hours a day.
>
> "I was bombarded by so many fund-raisers that I could have gone to five a week," Gotbaum recalls. "But it was frustrating. I was writing out checks but feeling no attachment or connection to the causes I was writing them for."
>
> During the summer of 1986, a number of the founders who called themselves Amherst friends energetically scouted out service organizations and volunteer clearinghouses. Their objective was to identify organizations that would provide volunteers with a sense of community, with reinforcement, and, if need be, with rudimentary training. Also, the organizations should be sufficiently flexible to accommodate young professionals with very demanding work schedules. At sum-

mer's end, Gotbaum says, they were convinced that no such organization existed in New York City. They would have to form their own.

Tax-exempt and nonprofit, New York Cares has never advertised for new members. Still, about 75 people seek it out each month. As of June 1989, there were about 900 active members working in partnership with about 50 nonprofit organizations around the city. Among those organizations are City Volunteer Corps Tutoring Program, Dorot (visits the homebound elderly), East Harlem Tutorial Program, God's Love, We Deliver (provides meals to people with AIDS), Habitat for Humanity, and the Jewish Home and Hospital for the Aged.

A handful of major New York banks and insurance companies now reward employee volunteer service with sabbatical leaves, and Ken Adams has begun to raise funds for New York Cares by charging corporations a consulting fee for organizing in-house volunteer programs.

Gotbaum is not surprised by this crescendo of volunteer activity. " 'Yuppie' was a bum rap," he says of the disdainful epithet and its presumption that young upwardly mobile professionals are apathetic about the needs of the less fortunate. "People just needed to get involved" (p. 10)

Well, what has happened since the founding of New York Cares and since Allen's article in *Amherst*? New York Cares published *Project Calendar January 1995*, which reveals some exciting growth while pointing out the ongoing challenges of voluntarism.

The *Project Calendar* leads off:

New York Cares has a wide variety of volunteer projects that need your help: small teams, large teams, individual projects, one-day projects, and special projects. Remember, to volunteer with New York Cares, you must first attend an orientation meeting.

After these very directed messages, the *Project Calendar* rhetorically asks:

What will you do this year? New York Cares had a banner year in 1994. We oriented more new volunteers than ever before. In an average month 3,000 volunteers roll up their sleeves to do hands-on service. Despite all of our success, we face a serious challenge. There is no shortage of new volunteers

... yet more and more frequently we struggle to fill volunteer projects. We need to hear from all of you: "What is going on?"

One of the things that makes New York Cares so attractive to so many people is the flexibility of our program and the varying levels of commitment. We can offer this flexibility because of the consistent corps of volunteers who serve regularly. However, when that corps stops growing, or even diminishes, we have a serious gap to fill.

We know you're out there, and we know you're committed to community service because you have already come to orientation. But, think for a moment, when was the last time you volunteered? What would you like to see in the calendar that isn't currently being offered? How can we work together to improve New York Cares?

The innovation of New York Cares is that it focuses on giving young professionals a meaningful relationship with a community service organization while serving as partner and volunteer broker to such extant agencies as St. John the Divine, the Village Temple, the Harlem United Community AIDS Center, and others.

In essence, New York Cares is a distribution system similar to that provided by a travel agency in the corporate sector. Rather than create a new organization that provides a new array of programs and services, New York Cares has identified those community service organizations that are of interest to its particular cohort of young professional volunteers and has provided the training and venue for those young professionals to hook up with the nonprofits that have particular relevance to them.

These three cases provide hands-on examples of reengineering the role and responsibility of volunteers. Indeed, some might argue that President Clinton's Corporation for National Service is a new paradigm of voluntarism. Others are most concerned about the negative impact such a program will have on the nonprofit sector. This federally sponsored corporation is modeled after the Peace Corps and provides opportunities for Americans to serve primarily in the fields of education, the environment, and police training. These Americorps "volunteers" receive a $7,225 annual stipend plus up to $9,540 over two years toward the cost of higher education. This equates to $7 an hour, not including health and child care benefits, which are provided through Americorps. Only time will tell if this is a boon or bane to the concept of voluntarism. In our view, this is not a volunteer effort as the participants are paid, albeit a meager amount. It is more akin to an internship program and should be so recognized.

CHECKLIST FOR SUCCESS

As we indicated at the outset of this chapter, there are growing numbers of organizations that are beginning to deal aggressively and intentionally with the development of new volunteer paradigms. Based on our own experience as well as that of your nonprofit colleagues, we urge you to

- Assess the volunteer base that has and continues to serve your organization through a stakeholder analysis, a stratification assessment, and a demographic assessment.
- Conduct the same analysis of those cohorts you have identified as volunteer prospects.
- Make volunteer training and development mandatory (see Chapter 6 for details).
- Provide current and prospective volunteers not only with a keen sense of mission and vision of your organization but also with a sense of community with one another.
- Reinforce and celebrate publicly and privately the special gifts of time and money volunteers bring to your nonprofit.
- Provide a personally meaningful if not riveting experience for the volunteer.
- Reach out to youngsters, their families, and their friends in order to develop a familylike network, enthusiasm, and commitment.
- Provide flexible schedules/opportunities for volunteers of all ages to accommodate work schedules, day care parameters, and the schedules and transportation needs of those who are elderly or retired.
- Be intentional about the volunteer profile you seek.
- Reach out to persons of color and other underrepresented populations your organization might serve but who have not been historically welcomed into your volunteer network.
- Make it easy for the volunteer to find your organization and get involved. Publish up-to-date schedules about where volunteer help is required, the time required to fulfill the assignment, and the timetable for the assignment.
- Value and cherish each and every volunteer as you would a staff member (see Chapter 6).

CHAPTER FIVE

The Duty of Stewardship

In the previous chapter, we talked about the volunteer who provides service and care and donates time. This chapter focuses specifically on the volunteer at the board level, commonly referred to as a *trustee, director,* or *board member,* and the collective of individual trustees and directors that comprises the board.

The initial section of this chapter focuses on the moral imperative of trusteeship or what we describe as the *duty of stewardship.* Unfortunately, the recent experiences of venerable organizations such as the United Way of America and the National Association for the Advancement of Colored People (NAACP) point to the fallibility of the nonprofit sector as a whole and of its boards and directors in particular. There is, in this arena, no surer way for the nonprofit sector to implode than through dereliction of duty.

The second section of this chapter talks about the role of governing boards and the standards of nonprofit governance that have been developed by the external agencies that function as the watchdogs of the nonprofit sector. The balance of this chapter talks about ways to conduct a governance self-assessment and reengineer those roles, relationships, and responsibilities that may be problematic for your nonprofit's board, given today's environment and the unfortunate circumstances that have plagued a number of small and large organizations. This part of the chapter provides you with the work plan and tools to conduct such a self-assessment and make the changes necessary for a well-ordered board.

THE MORAL IMPERATIVE OF TRUSTEESHIP

Of the millions of Americans who serve as volunteers, 1.3% (see Exhibit 4–2), are classified as board members or trustees. This small cadre is responsible for the legal and fiduciary oversight of an economy of immense proportion, yet there is no deep-seated personal or collective understanding of what it means to be a director.

In 1983, the Association of Governing Boards in Washington, D.C. published *The Good Steward: A Guide to Theological School Trusteeship*. This resource guide for the trustees and senior staff of theological schools in the United States and Canada marked the culmination of a thirty-month study sponsored by the Lilly Endowment. It was the first time that such an intensive and inclusive review of trusteeship had been undertaken on behalf of theological education.

As the years have passed, experience tells us that *The Good Steward* was and is still right on target. What Larry L. Greenfield says about the ephemeral qualities of trusteeship in his chapter, "Trusteeship and Administration," can be summed up in two key concepts:

1. The "deepest meaning of trusteeship is religious.... All human beings are entrusted with a responsibility to care for the gifts God has given." In that sense, we are all "trustees."

2. "The larger significance of trusteeship cannot be understood apart from the rich overtones of such enduring notions as 'ministry' and 'vocation.' " "Those who do accept the role and responsibility of trustee are, in fact, called to ministry."

Although Greenfield's comments may sound too fundamentalist from a religious perspective, it is true now, more than ever, that trusteeship needs necessarily to be a higher calling or as Richard T. Ingram said in the foreword of *The Good Steward*: "While holding a trusteeship continues to be an honor, it is far from honorary."

This chapter's title grows out of our deep-seated conviction about the duty or moral imperative of being designated trustee or director.

CASE STUDY

Reengineering Board Roles, Responsibilities, and Procedures

In the February 22, 1995, *Wall Street Journal*, p. B1 Pamela Sebastian reports:

> "The Aramony situation has served as a catalyst for the United Way of America and for all other nonprofits to look closely at their performance and review processes," says Keith Bailey ... chairman-elect of the United Way of America Board of Governors. "Everyone is affected by it. You don't have to be the one in the spotlight," he says.

Since 1992, the United Way of America has revamped its governance structure and has taken steps to improve financial and ethical accountability and achieve broader member representation. Among those steps, it has increased the number of board members from 37 to 45, one-third of whom now directly represent local United Ways; added six board committees responsible for areas like budget and finance; developed a code of ethics; and put more rigorous financial controls in place.

The United Way of America has been cooperating with a separate review of its governance procedures by the New York state attorney general, which oversees the New York–chartered nonprofit.

The scandal has sparked soul-searching elsewhere in the nonprofit community. The National Charities Information Bureau is preparing a booklet on what should be in a typical conflict-of-interest policy, and the National Center for Nonprofit Boards recently compiled its first national survey of governance policies and issues.

Meanwhile, the spending scandal has forced executives to view board memberships less as honorary posts and more as jobs requiring considerable time and energy. "Now, many more people consider (directorships) more seriously," says Nancy Axelrod, President of the National Center for Nonprofit Boards in Washington, D.C. "Prospective nonprofit directors want to know more clearly what will be expected of them in terms of time, responsibility, and performance evaluation," she says.

THE ROLE OF THE GOVERNING BOARD

The governing board represents the pinnacle of volunteer involvement. Unlike the volunteer who provides hands-on assistance at the operational level of the nonprofit, the volunteer as director and trustee holds in trust the nonprofit's financial, human resource, and physical assets. To that end, the individual director and the collective or board is responsible for hiring and evaluating the executive director and for ensuring that an ongoing strategic planning and resource allocation process is in place. The board is also responsible for ensuring sound policy guidance and recruiting, nominating, and selecting individual directors who are of the highest moral character. Exhibit 5–1 enumerates what your nonprofit's board should be doing.

- Selecting and evaluating the executive director, and, if necessary, replacing the incumbent.
- Preparing a working agenda and set of performance expectations that will permit the executive director to lead effectively.
- Clarifying the organization's mission and ensuring that a sound strategic planning process and plan are in place with the appropriate evaluation/performance criteria.
- Ensuring that the financial, human resource, and physical assets of the organization are well cared for and support the goals and objectives articulated in the strategic plan.
- Ensuring that the nonprofit operates efficiently and effectively and in a socially and morally responsible manner.
- Ensuring sound policy development and implementation.
- Ensuring the organization's survival with a legal duty to conserving and protecting the assets of the organization, not only money, property, and lives but also the goodwill and integrity of the organization.
- Building a conscientious, committed, moral, and mission-passionate board in which
  - the members are informed about the nonprofit as a whole and the role of its particular organization within the larger context of the nonprofit sector
  - the chair of the board and the executive director are working partners
  - the board agenda is long range and has a focused, strategic thrust
  - board size and composition are appropriate to the governance task at hand
  - board committee structure is chartered and organized for results
  - board meetings are not only interesting and effective but provide the venue for directors and senior staff alike to grow professionally and personally
  - the nominating process intentionally ferrets out people who have the moral attributes to serve as stewards; the requisite management and programmatic skills; the capacity to provide financial resources personally or to gain access to those resources; the intestinal fortitude to make difficult decisions; the organization's rather than their own best interests at heart; and who represent the demography of the country, the region, or the populations served with particular commitment to women and people of color
  - the board development committee recruits, nominates, trains, develops, and evaluates individual director performance and makes abundantly clear the particular job or contract the incumbent has as director

Exhibit 5–1 Checklist of Board Responsibilities
Source: Standards in Philanthropy: The National Charities Information Bureau.

1. *Board Governance*—The board sets policy, establishes and enforces fiscal guidelines, and performs on-going governance of the entity. As part of its due diligence, the board should regularly review its organization's policies, programs, and operations. Specifically, the board should have:
   - an independent, volunteer membership;
   - an independent, volunteer membership;
   - a minimum of 5 voting members;
   - an individual attendance policy;
   - specific terms of office for its officers and members;
   - in-person, face-to-face meetings, at least twice a year, evenly spaced, with a majority of voting members in attendance at each meeting;
   - no fees to members for board service, but payments may be made for costs as a result of board participation;
   - no more than one paid staff member, usually the chief staff officer, who shall not chair the board or serve as treasurer;
   - policy guidelines to avoid material conflicts of interest involving board or staff;
   - no material conflicts of interest involving board or staff; and
   - a policy promoting pluralism and diversity within the organization's board, staff, and constituencies.
2. *Purpose*—The organization's purpose, approved by the board, should be formally and specifically articulated.
3. *Programs*—The organization's activities should be consistent with its statement of purpose/mission.
4. *Information*—Promotion, fund-raising, and public information should describe accurately the organization's identity, purpose, programs, and financial needs.
5. *Financial Support and Related Activities*—The board is accountable for all authorized activities generating financial support on the organization's behalf.
   - Fund raising activities should encourage voluntary giving and should not apply unwarranted pressure.
   - Descriptive and financial information for all substantial income and for all revenue-generating activities conducted by the organization should be disclosed on request.
   - Basic descriptive and financial information for income derived from authorized commercial activities involving the organization's name and which are conducted by for-profit organizations should be available. All public promotion of such commercial activity should either include this information or indicate that it is available from the organization.
6. *Use of Funds*—The organization's use of funds should reflect consideration of current and future needs and resources in planning for program continuity. Specifically, the organization should:

– spend at least 60% of annual expenses for program activities;

– insure that fund-raising expenses, in relation to fund-raising results, are reasonable over time;

– have net assets available for the following fiscal year that, usually, are not more than twice the current year's expenses or the next year's budget, which ever is higher; and

– not have a persistent and/or increasing deficit in the unrestricted fund balance.

7. *Annual Reporting*—An annual report should be available upon request and should include:

– an explicit narrative description of the organization's major activities, presented in the same major categories and covering the same fiscal period as the audited financial statements;

– a list of board members;

– audited financial statements, or at a minimum, a comprehensive financial summary that (1) identifies all revenues in significant categories; (2) reports expenses in the same program, management/general, and fund-raising categories as in the audited financial statements; and (3) reports all ending balances.

8. *Accountability*—An organization should supply on request complete financial statements which:

– are prepared in conformity with generally accepted accounting principles (GAAP), accompanied by a report of an independent certified public accountant, and reviewed by the board;

– fully disclose financial resources and obligations, including transactions with related parties and affiliated organizations, significant events affecting finances and significant categories of income and expense;

– provide a statement of functional allocation of expenses in addition to such statements required by GAAP to be included in the financial statements; and

– combined financial statements for a national organization with affiliates prepared in the foregoing manner.

9. *Budget*—The organization should prepare a detailed annual budget consistent with the major classifications in the audited financial statements and approved by the board.

Exhibit 5–2 Standards in Philanthropy.
Source: The National Charities Information Bureau, © 1988.

The checklist of roles and responsibilities should serve to formulate your nonprofit's generic position description for current and prospective directors. It should also be used to educate your staff about the duties of stewardship.

These roles and responsibilities need to be clearly understood and actualized individually and collectively by the board of directors as these duties provide the framework against which your organization is evaluated by such external watchdog groups as the National Charities Information Bureau, the Council of Better Business Bureaus, and various accrediting and certification agencies.

STANDARDS OF NONPROFIT GOVERNANCE

Nonprofit governing boards are expected to meet the standards established by the National Charities Information Bureau. This bureau, founded in 1918, is an association supported by concerned contributors that provides reports and advisory services about national and international nonprofit organizations that solicit contributions from the public (i.e., organizations that deal with national health and welfare, veterans, foreign relief, and the like). Nonprofit governing boards are answerable to the public as they solicit funds from the general public based on public trust.

The National Charities Information Bureau recommends and applies the nine standards enumerated in Exhibit 5–2 as common measures of governance and management.

The Council of Better Business Bureaus (CBBB), a nonprofit entity, was established in 1970 to serve and educate the consumer, establish voluntary self-regulation of national advertising, settle consumer complaints through arbitration, and provide prepurchase information to consumers. The CBBB is supported by 240,000 business and professional firms in all fields and 200 local BBBs in the United States. The council has established Standards for Charitable Solicitations under the three general headings of governance, use of funds, and public accountability. Exhibit 5–3 provides the detail.

The standards established by the National Charities Information Bureau and the Council of Better Business Bureaus are critical because they provide the fundamental framework within which nonprofits must operate. Noncompliance with these standards could subject nonprofits to a federal and/or state evaluation. The bureaus, with the support of the government, will help guide a nonprofit that is not in compliance with the nine standards back to full reinstatement.

Equally as important, these standards should serve as your own nonprofit's checklist for reengineering policies, procedures, processes, and systems that are not in conformance with these nationally held standards. The case study we provide points dramatically to what damage can be done to a nonprofit organization as an entity as well as to its board and individual directors if due diligence is not exercised by the board, its chair, and its executive director.

1. *Governance*
   - Soliciting organizations shall have an adequate governance structure.
   - Soliciting organizations shall have an active governing body.
   - Soliciting organizations shall have an independent governing body.
2. *Use of Funds*
   - At least 50% of total income from all sources shall be applied to programs and activities directly related to the purposes for which the organization exists.
   - At least 50% of public contributions shall be applied to programs and activities described in solicitations, in accordance with donor expectations.
   - Fund-raising costs shall not exceed 35% of related contributions.
   - Total fund-raising and administrative costs shall not exceed 50% of total income.
   - Soliciting organizations shall substantiate on request their application of funds, in accordance with donor expectations, to the programs and activities described in solicitation.
   - Soliciting organizations shall establish and exercise adequate controls over disbursements.
3. *Public Accountability*
   - Soliciting organizations shall provide an annual report on request.
   - Soliciting organizations shall provide complete annual financial statements upon request.
   - The soliciting organization's financial statements shall present adequate information to serve as a basis for informed decisions.
   - Organizations receiving a substantial portion of their income through the fundraising activities of controlled or affiliated entities shall provide on request an accounting of all income received by and fundraising costs incurred by such entities.

Exhibit 5–3   Standards for Charitable Solicitations
Source: © The Council of Better Business Bureaus, Arlington, VA.

CASE STUDY

The Damage Caused by a Board Chair

The February 23, 1995, issue of the *Chronicle of Philanthropy* summarizes the problems facing the NAACP at that time:

- Allegations from angry board members that the board chairman, Dr. William F. Gibbons, had misused the association's funds. They charged in a federal lawsuit that the chairman, in concert with the chief executive, was responsible for the improper spending of at least $1.4 million in pension funds and $440,000 in restricted grant funds.

- Excessive use of the chairman's American Express card, with nearly $500,000 rung up since 1986; receipt of $300,000 in checks for unexplained reimbursements from the NAACP.

- An unauthorized loan of $10,000 for Dr. Gibbons, the board chairman.

- Accusations from members of the NAACP as well as dissenting board members that the board had shirked its fiduciary responsibility by failing to act in a timely basis concerning its financial crisis.

- Difficulty convincing foundations that the NAACP would use grant money responsibly.

- A threat from a prominent NAACP member and former assistant director, Michael Meyers, to ask the New York attorney general to investigate the organization and remove the board if necessary.

In a contentious meeting held on February 18, 1995, Myrlie Evers-Williams was elected chairwoman of the board. Despite Ms. Evers-Williams's one-vote winning margin, people within the organization are hopeful that she will be able to use her impressive people and management skills and correct this painful and problematic situation for the board and for the organization as a whole. Fundamentally, Ms. Evers-Williams and the new executive director of the organization will have to redesign the way in which the board as a whole and its individual directors comply with the standards set out by the National Charities Information Bureau and the Better Business Bureau. In addition, Ms. Evers-Williams and the board will have to define a new infrastructure (policies, processes, and systems) that will inform them of what is happening at the national and local levels of the organization so that they will be able to make informed and timely decisions. Further, the role of the new executive director and the new board chairwoman must be clearly defined and articulated.

THE ABCs OF GOVERNANCE

A review and self-assessment of both individual directors/trustees and the board as a whole should be a routine discipline for your organization. Such an approach, applied on an annual basis, will enable you to assess the ability of individual directors and the board as a whole to meet the myriad of requirements of sound stewardship. Experience suggests that such self-assessment seldom, if rarely, occurs. Such self-assessment should address basic board policies and procedures, including

- Bylaws and articles of incorporation
- Understanding by the directors/trustees of their role and responsibilities
- Performance of directors in fulfilling the mandates and objectives of their strategic and resource allocation processes
- Relationship of the board to advisory and visiting committees, as well as other local boards or the national board
- Committee structure of the board
- Record keeping and related practices of the board
- Conduct of board meetings and board business
- Distinction between those areas reserved for staff and those reserved for the board

We recommend that you establish an ad hoc committee of your board or utilize the nominating and/or board development committee to conduct such a review. We urge you to include your organization's executive director in the self-assessment and to conduct the self-assessment in a retreat-like setting. We are certain that you will learn much from this interaction that, in turn, will allow you to reengineer the manner in which governance functions for your organization.

Such reengineering can come in many forms. From the perspective of the organization of the board, the number of committees, committee roles and responsibilities, and the relationship of the board to the national organization's board or to other chapter/affiliate boards may warrant redesigning. From the perspective of policies and procedures, the board may decide to redefine major policy, delineate and clarify the role of staff (in particular the executive director) in the day-to-day management of the nonprofit versus the policy prerogatives of the board and redesign the way in which it hires and fires its executive director. From the perspective of administrative processes, the board may decide to reengineer the way in which board business is conducted; minutes are distributed and approved; committee reports, including the strategic plan and budget, are distributed and approved; or how the recruiting and nominating process for directors is conducted. The fourth element of reengineering, technology, may create an entire rethinking of the way in which the board conducts its business. For examples, can trustees have access to the nonprofits network and E-mail? Can video conferencing be introduced to facilitate the work of committees? What governance reports should be generated to support the work of the directors?

We encourage you to utilize the Governance Self-Assessment Worksheet we have developed (Exhibit 5–4). This worksheet is the result of years of work with various nonprofit entities and the particular pressures that boards and their members experience at this most stressful time.

FACTORS COMPLICATING THE ABCs OF GOVERNANCE

Many factors complicate governance self-assessment. Several, however, are critical to grasp. One is the evolutionary nature of boards and the impact this necessarily has on the ability of a board to respond to change. Additionally, Exhibit 5–5 portrays how governance structures tend to change over time as their particular organization evolves. This paradigm is contained in Richard T. Ingram's *Ten Basic Responsibilities of Nonprofit Boards*, published by the National Center for Nonprofit Boards in 1991.

Experience tells us that organizations and boards are often not in sync developmentally. For example, a nonprofit may have evolved from its grass-roots founding thirty years ago into a $30 million national health organization, but its board is still predominantly peopled with caregivers who started the organization and a handful of directors with national prominence as fund-raisers and corporate CEOs. Therefore, the national significance of the organization is not matched by a board of national caliber.

Another example of the evaluation of nonprofit organization governance has to do with the expectation of directors as those who "give, get, or get off." In the early years of a nonprofit, a modest or low expectation exists for directors to make annual personal contributions or raise funds. As the organization grows and develops an outstanding reputation for program and service delivery, a clear expectation arises for directors to make annual personal contributions (give) and to participate in fund-raising (get).

In addition, three special circumstances further complicate governance and board assessment. First, many nonprofits have legal or informal relationships with other nonprofit and for-profit entities. Second, some boards are multitiered. That is, they have a parent board and a local boards(s). Third, advisory boards, visiting committees, and auxiliary boards are sometimes created to identify persons with certain professional proficiency who could be of technical assistance to the nonprofit. They also could recognize donor largesse.

I. *Mission, Vision, and Policy*

- ❑ Are the mission and vision statements relevant?
- ❑ Has the board had ample opportunity to review them? Do they serve to guide the work of the board in determining organizational policy?
- ❑ Does the board help to determine what programs and services should be maintained, be divested, or receive an infusion of resources?
- ❑ How do board members know that their organization has in fact delivered mission-based programs and services to multiple constituents?

SUMMARY: How have we as a board done overall in this category?

II. *Strategic Planning and Resource Allocation*

- ❑ When was the last time the board was involved in a organization-wide strategic planning process?
- ❑ Is there an established cycle for planning and resource allocation? Is there a monitoring and control cycle that has been established?
- ❑ Does the board agenda periodically call on the senior staff to report progress?

SUMMARY: Overall, do you believe that the board is adequately versed in the mission and vision to respond to major strategic and resource allocation issues confronting the entity as a whole?

III. *Capital Planning and Asset Management*

- ❑ Is the board sensitive about the relationship of the physical plant with senior staff attempts to develop a sense of community?
- ❑ Is the board aware of the on-going impact of technology on the charity's capital and physical plant budget?
- ❑ Is there an approved master plan?
- ❑ Does the board have the knowledge to discern when new capital construction and/or renovation projects are appropriate?
- ❑ Is the board too involved in the day-to-day management of the charity's custodial, maintenance, and utilities operations?
- ❑ Has the board done everything it could to avoid a potential conflict of interest between a vendor/contractor and the director?

SUMMARY: Many board members are in the business of real estate, plant operations and property management. Are their firms or the firms of friends involved in the day-to-day aspects of these operations? Do such trustees benefit financially from such a relationship?

IV. *Fiduciary Responsibility*

- ❑ Does the board fully understand its role in developing financial policies, and managing investments?
- ❑ Does the board have ample time to review budget proposals and monitor the current year's budget?
- ❑ In addition to having the requisite skills to manage the financial assets of the organization, does the board have the capacity to contribute to the organization?

❑ Is there adequate financial commitment from individual board members to give personally or influence others to give?

❑ Is there an adequate development and fund-raising department in the organization? Is there a coordinated effort among the chair of the board, the executive director, and the senior development/fund-raising officer?

SUMMARY: Is the board fully aware of the organization's financial condition?

V.   *Board Membership*

❑ Do you believe that current board members are sufficiently committed to the mission and vision of your organization?

❑ Do you have the systems and mechanisms in place to identify and attract prospective board members?

❑ Does the board have persons with backgrounds in one or more of the following areas?

– management

– human resources

– fund-raising and development

– investment

– real estate, construction, property management

– law

– professional training apropos to the programs and services offered by your organization

– public relations/marketing

– hospitality industry (food service, travel hotels)

❑ Does the board strive to reach out and establish relationships with diverse groups that support the organization's mission? Is there evidence that the board intentionally wants to become inclusive and that it truly values diversity?

❑ Is the board's composition adequate with respect to

– age

– gender

– persons of color

– geography

❑ Are the board's policies and practices appropriate with respect to

– the clarity of trustee role and responsibility

– length and number of successive trustee terms

– age limit

– honorary titles, such as *emeritus*

– size of the board

– the provision of director's and officer's liability insurance to mitigate personal trustee liability

❑ Is there an orientation program for new and continuing board members?

❏ Are individual trustees/directors reviewed on an annual basis? What about the chair and the officers?

SUMMARY: Do we have the right people on the board? Are they onboard for the right reason?

VI. *Board Organization*

❏ Within the past two years, has the board reviewed the existing committee structure and bylaws of the board?

❏ Are board materials of the appropriate summary level? Are they forwarded sufficiently in advance of committee and full board meetings?

❏ Are agendas focused on policy or day-to-day management issues?

❏ Are the number and duration of board meetings sufficient for the conduct of board business?

❏ Does the board chair and the organization's executive director partner in the preparation of board/committee agendas?

❏ Is the chair effective in the conduct of board business? Are the board meetings meaningful to individual board members or are they merely obligatory gatherings?

❏ Is the present committee structure appropriate or would the board be more effective if it acted as a committee of the whole?

❏ Is the executive committee too powerful? Does it consult and inform the full board of its actions, or does it function fairly independently?

❏ Does the committee structure address the basics of governance (finance, audit, investments, strategic planning, nominating, and board development) while simultaneously addressing the mission of the organization (programs, services, educational programs, advocacy, etc.)?

❏ Are there too many committees?

❏ Is there a venue by which the voices of constituencies and stakeholders can be heard prior to board action?

❏ Do board policies allow for sufficient rotation of leadership to retain trustee interest and commitment?

SUMMARY: Overall, is the board organized to support the mission and vision of the organization in the most effective, efficient, and caring manner possible?

VII. *Board/Chief Executive Partnership*

❏ Has the board, in conjunction with the executive director, developed a written statement depicting the roles and responsibilities of the chair's executive director?

❏ Is this written statement/contract updated on an annual basis and does it serve as the basis for annual performance evaluation?

❏ Has the board delegated sufficient authority and responsibility to the executive director to manage successfully?

❏ Is there mutual trust and respect between the board and the executive director?

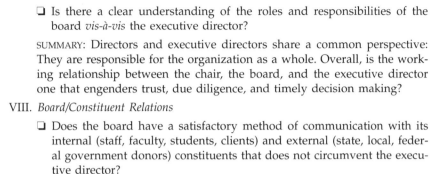

❏ Is there a clear understanding of the roles and responsibilities of the board *vis-à-vis* the executive director?

SUMMARY: Directors and executive directors share a common perspective: They are responsible for the organization as a whole. Overall, is the working relationship between the chair, the board, and the executive director one that engenders trust, due diligence, and timely decision making?

VIII. *Board/Constituent Relations*

❏ Does the board have a satisfactory method of communication with its internal (staff, faculty, students, clients) and external (state, local, federal government donors) constituents that does not circumvent the executive director?

❏ Does the board, through the office of the executive director, reach out to constituents to ensure the ongoing development, implementation, delivery, and evaluation of programs and services?

❏ Has the board adopted policies relevant to the constituents it serves, how it is to serve them, and what is provided with respect to programs and services?

❏ Are there grievance, due process, and other enumerated procedures that stipulate the board's role as the court of last resort?

SUMMARY: How well equipped is the board to deal with the multiple constituents it serves? How effectively does it coordinate these efforts with those of the executive director?

Exhibit 5–4   Governance Self-Assessment Worksheet

In the case of nonprofits with a legal or informal relationship with another entity, it is critical that the board ask itself some fundamental questions about the nature, scope, and purpose of such a relationship:

– Are the interests of our particular board being heard by the parent agency, the denomination, the particular coalition, or the system of higher education?

– Have there been conflicts between the best interests of our organization and those of our market sector (social services, health care, etc.) as represented by our designated umbrella organization (e.g., National Health Council)?

– Do the conventions we attend of various constituent or umbrella groups provide us with an understanding of what the sector is confronting? In turn, does that group or umbrella organization advocate adequately on our behalf and in the best interest of our organization's mission?

Governance structures tend to change over time as organizations evolve from . . .

From		To
founding		regional or national significance
small numbers of constituencies (or members)		extensive numbers of constituencies
small budgets and staffs		extensive budgets and staffs
small boards		large boards
use of the title of "executive director" for the chief staff officer		use of the title of "president" for the chief staff officer
use of the title of "president" for the chief volunteer officer		use of the title of "chair", "chairman", or "chairperson" for the chief volunteer officer
boards that operate as committees of the whole		boards that depend on effective standing committee

From		To
founders who eliminate board membership (little turnover)		directors chosen on merit, background, skills (reasonable turnover)
high dependence on directors who also serve as grass-roots volunteers		less dependence on directors who also serve as grass-roots volunteers
directors who "represent" constituencies		directors who are selected "at large"
strong emotional commitment by directors to organization purposes		less emotional investment and more use of directors' expertise, skills, and influence
modest or no expectation for directors to make annual personal contributions or raise funds		clear expectation for directors to make annual personal contributions (to serve as an example to others) and to participate in fundraising

Exhibit 5–5 A Paradigm: The Evolution of Nonprofit Organization Governance

– Do our grass-roots supporters understand that it is important for our organization and its board to be involved in the greater non-profit marketplace so that our collective voice is heard?

Although many examples may be cited, we draw upon the Alzheimer's Association and its active participation in the National Health Council.

CASE STUDY

Joining Together for the Greater Good

As far as nonprofit organizations go, the Alzheimer's Association is a fledgling group. This thirty-year-old organization has an enviable record of growth. It has been successful in heightening public awareness about the disease and related disorders; developing model programs for the education and training of caregivers; monitoring medical advances and investing in breakthrough research; and providing advocacy in the areas of long-term care, health reform, and federal medical and health services research support.

The Alzheimer's Association is a member of the National Health Council, the seventy-five-year-old organization founded as a clearinghouse and advocacy organization to promote and support voluntary health agencies that engage individuals, families, and communities across the nation to volunteer in the effort to prevent, treat, and cure debilitating and life-threatening illnesses, chronic health conditions, and physical and developmental disabilities. The forty-one voluntary health agency members (organizations such as the American Cancer Society, March of Dimes Birth Defects Foundation, and National Multiple Sclerosis are also members), which are a part of this umbrella organization, address diseases and disorders afflicting more than 130 million Americans.

In addition to these forty-one members, the National Health Council boasts members from professional and trade groups such as the American Medical and American Hospital Associations; twenty-two businesses, such as Warner-Lambert, Merck, Aetna, and CIGNA; twenty health-related nonprofit organizations, such as Save the Children Federation, the American Association of Retired People, and United Way; and five governmental agencies such as HCFA and the Social Security Administration.

The resulting critical mass of nonprofit organizations, professional and trade groups, businesses, and governmental agencies enables the individual organizations to influence advocacy, research, and program and service delivery mechanisms for all health-related organizations in a forceful and unified manner. It also fosters inter-locking working relationships between and among staff of the National Health Council and its for-profit and nonprofit member organizations.

The second complex board scenario deals with those charities, like the US Committee for UNICEF, that have multitiered boards. This is especially true of those national nonprofits that have local affiliates but whose local boards function under the umbrella of the governing body of the national organization.

CASE STUDY

Distinguishing the Role of a National Governing Board from That of the Local Volunteer Leadership Team

The board of directors of the U.S. Committee for UNICEF has a set of bylaws, articles of incorporation, and other legal documents that entrust it with the health, welfare, and effective stewardship of the organization's resources. The U.S. Committee has offices staffed full-time in New York City, Atlanta, Chicago, Houston, and Los Angeles. Each of the local boards has its own focus and vision in support of the overall mission of the U.S. Committee for UNICEF.

As an example, the mission statement articulated by the Los Angeles Leadership Team (the local board) and the staff is: "In order to expand our fundraising base and to increase public awareness of UNICEF's work in the developing world, we will seek to establish closer ties and collaborate with local children's groups toward the development and promotion of children's well-being."

When Marilyn Solomon, executive director of the Los Angeles–based operation, started her work, she reached out to her Los Angeles board to expand this base to include a cadre of racially and ethnically diverse women and men. Rather than continue to call this corps of volunteers a board, Ms. Solomon and her directors collectively came up with the phrase Los Angeles Leadership Team. This helped to distinguish their modus operandi from both the National Advisory Committee comprised of prominent church leaders, government leaders, and others committed to the welfare of children in developing countries that provides counsel to the national organization's president on issues related to education, advocacy, and fund-raising and from the national governing body or board of directors.

Because the national board serves as the governing board, the Los Angeles corps of volunteers believed it critical to distinguish clearly its advisory and fund-raising role from that of a governance role. While creating this innovative concept of a leadership team, Ms. Solomon and her key volunteers undertook the following assessment to ensure they would reengineer their role appropriately:

- With this new paradigm, will there be a clearer understanding of the role and responsibilities of our team *vis-à-vis* the national board concerning governance of the organization?
- Are the members of our team satisfied that they have the authority to carry out their work at the local level without being second-guessed at the national board level?
- Has any member of the national board contravened any recommendation or action of our team? Do we have the proper safeguards in place to ensure that this does not arbitrarily take place in the future?
- Is there a climate of mutual trust and respect between our local team and the national board?

In the third case, when there are advisory committees, visiting committees, or auxiliary boards, the roles and responsibilities of these volunteer entities must once again be distinguished from those of the governing board. We use an example from higher education as this sector of the nonprofit often embraces this approach.

For many nonprofits, such nongoverning groups provide an opportunity to publicly recognize the largesse of donors, to utilize the expertise of nationally recognized professionals, and to train prospective directors and trustees for membership to the governing board. Once again, we recommend that you undertake the governance self-assessment (see Exhibit 5–4) for each of the volunteer entities and the governing board.

CASE STUDY

Training Ground for Governing Board Membership

Clark University, a private institution of higher learning in Worcester, Massachusetts, is known as the home of John Goddard and the Freud Lectures. Started as a graduate institution, it is now a small university with an intense, undergraduate curriculum, as well as many world-class graduate programs. It has the honor of being a member of the prestigious Association of American Universities, which includes among its ranks such institutions as Harvard, Yale, the University of California at Berkeley, and Princeton.

Clark's board of trustees is very clear about its stewardship role and is constantly provided educational and other material with which to thoughtfully conduct its fiscal and policy business. The goals and objectives of the advisory committee are clearly stipulated and communicated as is its role *vis-à-vis* the governing board, various women's fund-raising auxiliaries, and the numerous visiting committees that serve to evaluate the programmatic core of the university's academic offerings. The advisory committee is comprised of professionals with management and technical skills who serve for a period of two years and who come to campus twice a year to work with President Dr. Richard P. Traina and his senior staff on matters relating to learning, academic support services, enrollment management, and the like. These advisory committee meetings are roll-up-your-sleeves working sessions in which recommendations concerning program and administrative direction are made to the president and his senior staff.

In addition to this valuable input, the advisory board provides a venue in which the president can test an individual's commitment to the mission of the university and the interest that individual has in serving as a board member.

In short, the advisory committee provides a group of potential board members, immerses them in the specific issues facing Clark, and tests their commitment.

DISTINGUISHING THE CORPORATE FROM THE NONPROFIT BOARD

Nonprofit stewardship is a complex set of moral responsibilities set against a rigorous set of standards posed from without as well as from within the organization. Ironically, many of the women and men who sit on the boards of nonprofits—be they local or national, large or small— hail from the corporate sector. There are two qualities that distinguish the nonprofit from the for-profit sector that have relevance to stewardship: One is the fund accounting employed by nonprofit organizations and the other is the role and function of the board.

To the first point, nonprofit accounting is a foreign language to most directors who have been weaned on profit and loss statements; they are not trained or experienced in understanding endowments, funds functioning as endowments, an excess of expenditures over revenues, and other nonprofit-specific finance concepts. Worse, many of these incumbents are not willing to admit that they do not understand the fundamentals of fund accounting and, therefore, cannot properly read their own group's financial statements.

Second, although both profit and nonprofit boards have a common set of responsibilities, nonprofit boards possess some special qualities:

- They are mission based and constituency driven.
- Unlike their for-profit counterparts, which deal primarily with bottom-line performance, nonprofit boards spend little time assessing organizational and board performance.
- They spend considerable time mobilizing volunteers and fundraising.
- They exist for the public good and providing public service rather than generating profit.
- They are dependent on donations and are accountable to the general public they serve, unlike the for-profit sector, which lives by sales and profit margins and is answerable to investors and stockholders.
- Their focus is on a myriad of constituencies, among which are those who benefit from and those who support the organization. In the for-profit world, the primary constituent is the customer. Owners and the stockholders are the direct beneficiaries of the company's profit.
- Nonprofit boards are generally larger in order to enlist the views of its various constituencies and the different skill sets they require, as well as to enlist the support of influential donors. On the other hand, corporate boards are smaller and have identified people with the skills to contribute to the bottom line.

GUIDELINES TO LIVE BY WHILE REENGINEERING YOUR BOARD AND ITS PRACTICES

As you embark on reengineering your board and its practices:

- Put aside the ego satisfaction and the corrupting sense of power often associated with board membership and embrace a moral sensitivity of service and commitment to the nonprofit's mission.

- Ensure that your board has a written conflict-of-interest policy.
- Diversify board membership to include people of color, underrepresented groups, and women. Executive committees should reflect this diversity as well.
- Make sure that each and every board member understands the need to give, get, or get off.
- Be sanguine about the standards of governance established by watchdog agencies and be sure not only to meet but to exceed their expectations.
- Ensure that a working partnership develops between the board and the executive director.
- Remain steadfast about being a mission-based, constituency-driven charity and commit to it for the long term.
- Create a committee structure that mirrors the programs and services offered by your nonprofit and recognizes that a well-run and continually evaluated administrative infrastructure will ensure that the organization as well as the board will thrive.
- Ensure that the board has and continues to do its homework and can certify to those constituents it serves that the organization is on the right track.
- Never forget the need for ongoing director/trustee recruitment, retention, rotation, education, training, development, and recognition. Trustees/directors are people with the same developmental needs as staff.
- Ensure that there is an adequate infrastructure to support the work of the board. This means up-to-date policies and procedures, streamlined administrative processes, and technology to support communication and the dissemination of summarized management/governance reports.

CHAPTER SIX

Reengineering Volunteer and Staff Resources

"Of the best leader, when he is gone, they will say: We did it our-selves."

—Chinese proverb

"... whips and chains are no longer an alternative. Leaders must learn to change the nature of power and how it's employed."

—Warren Bennis, author of numerous leadership texts

"... we share as much information as we possibly can.... You cannot ask people to exercise broader judgment if their world is bounded by very narrow vision."

—Robert D. Haas, CEO, Levi Strauss

In this chapter, we make the case that reengineering is not simply new technology, redesigned processes, and streamlined policy and proce-dures manuals. Rather, reengineering is also the radical redesign of the way in which people—volunteers and staff—obtain and use knowl-edge to contribute productively to the mission of their organization.

Over the millennia, wise men and women have intuitively understood what makes people work harmoniously and productively in the family, in the extended community, and in the workplace. Unfortunately, however, the world is not sufficiently populated with the likes of Warren Bennis, Bob Haas, or the sage Chinese scholar. Indeed, what intuitively appears to some of us as common sense is a great threat to others who enjoy their self-perceived sense of power, rank, and place in the organizational hier-archy as well as lording over others whom they deem subordinate.

There is a further irony in the nonprofit world. Although 80% of the operating budgets of most nonprofits are directly attributable to total employee compensation costs (base salary plus benefits), the sector is woefully naive about what it takes to invest in people—be they volunteers or paid staff.

Small, sometimes nonexistent, budgets exist for staff and volunteer training and development at small and large organizations alike. A review of most operating budgets for museums, social service agencies, nongovernmental agencies, and performing arts organizations validates this statement. This is especially true of institutions of higher education, which assume that because so many of their staff (and faculty) hold the terminal degree (e.g. PhD, DBA etc) and are products of a rigorously defined discipline that they come automatically equipped to teach, conduct quality scholarly work, and perform community service functions.

What complicates the human resource component of the nonprofit even further is the presence of millions of volunteers who provide their labor free of charge. These contributed services, although critical and valuable, are not necessarily viewed realistically from a management perspective (see Chapter 4). Are we getting the most out of these volunteer efforts as we could be, given the value/cost paradox of volunteer efforts?

We begin this chapter with a brief discussion about management trends and human nature (for example, people saying one thing and doing another). The second section of this chapter focuses on the human spirit and what some managers in the world of the profit and the nonprofit have done to reengineer the organizational attitude toward human resources, making the workplace and work environment more humane and conducive to productivity.

Next, the current model for human resource management is described, followed by a discussion of what needs to occur to reengineer the way in which nonprofits manage their volunteer and staff resources. In the final sections of this chapter, we talk about new ways to design compensation systems that will support the new way of doing work that results from reengineering.

MANAGEMENT TRENDS AND HUMAN NATURE

The corporate world has been in the business of reengineering for a decade or so, and research demonstrates to those of us in the nonprofit sector what works and what doesn't. This is especially true of the research that focuses on the impact of reengineering on people at the most senior levels of the organization, those in the middle, and those at the entry and clerical levels—people are *the* constant in both sectors. Let's see what we can learn.

When you consider hiring a new nonsupervisory or production worker, how important are the following in your decision to hire?

(Ranked on scale of 1 through 5, with 1 being not important or not considered, and 5 being very important.)

Factor	Rank
Attitude	4.6
Communication skills	4.2
Previous work experience	4.0
Recommendations from current employees	3.4
Recommendations from previous employer	3.4
Industry-based credentials certifying skills	3.2
Years of schooling completed	2.9
Score on tests administered as part of interview	2.5
Academic performance (grades)	2.5
Experience or reputation of applicant's school	2.4
Teacher recommendations	2.1

Exhibit 6–1   Qualities That Count with Employers

Source: The New York Times National, February 20, 1995, p. A13. Survey developed by the National Center on the Educational Quality of the Work Force at the University of Pennsylvania NYT, Feb. 20, 1995 P. A13
(Figures from a Census Bureau survey of 3,000 employers nationwide, conducted in August and September 1994.)

Phrases such as *worker empowerment, valuing people as if they were assets,* and *recognizing the need for people skills* are currently in vogue among chief executives in the for-profit business community. Exhibit 6–1 enumerates what attributes are important to the chief executive in the for-profit workplace.

When 3,000 employers nationwide were recently queried about how important such factors as test scores, previous work experience, communication skills, attitudes, and so on were in hiring staff, attitude, communication skills, and previous work experience emerged as the top three of eleven factors. Although these responses indicate that this sample of employers appeared to value specific human attributes, other studies show a profound gap between rhetoric and reality. For example, a recent survey conducted by Towers Perrin, a consulting firm, indicates that nine out of ten senior executives reported that people were the most valuable company asset. Ninety-eight percent of those same respondents said improved employee performance would enhance the bottom line. Yet, when asked to rank the strategies most likely to yield success, these same executives put people and people-related issues—performance and investment in the workforce—near the bottom.

In fact, respondents ranked customer satisfaction, financial performance, and product and service quality as their three top priorities. Exhibit 6–2 illustrates the disconnection between the executive's belief in the mantra of customer satisfaction and his/her understanding of how important employees are to fulfilling customer satisfaction.

Patricia Milligan, a managing principal in Towers Perrin, provides her take on some of the survey results:

> The good news is that line executives, the ones closest to the customers, truly understand the relevance of managing their people. They are most likely to say it improves results. They are also the group most likely to correlate investment in people with business strategy. . . . If you look at how organizations downsize, they use appraisals that reflect past competencies, not the jobs and skills critical in the future.

Milligan's conclusions, as quoted by Barbara Presley Noble, are on target for the nonprofit too. Although most executive directors wax eloquent about how dependent their nonprofit is on its staff and volunteers, few have the will to look critically at the future and ask what jobs and skills are critical to the future. Indeed, most nonprofit organizations that have reengineered have failed to optimize such redesign because they have created new job descriptions with the proper empowerment and cross-functional work team concepts but have reassigned incumbents without the requisite training and development. The result is a volunteer and staff disconnection with the reengineered organization.

How can the nonprofit capture the human spirit in such a way as to make the operating environment more conducive to volunteers and staff productivity? Once again, it is time to learn some basics from our corporate counterparts.

THE HUMAN SPIRIT: LEARNING THE FUNDAMENTALS OF HUMAN RESOURCE MANAGEMENT

Managers in any sector who have a predilection for trust, honesty, respect, teamwork, and caring are among the most successful. Unfortu-

How executives assess the importance of key issues in determining business success, based on recent survey of 300 senior executives at mid-size and large companies. For example, more than 70% of the executives ranked customer satisfaction as among the three most important issues.

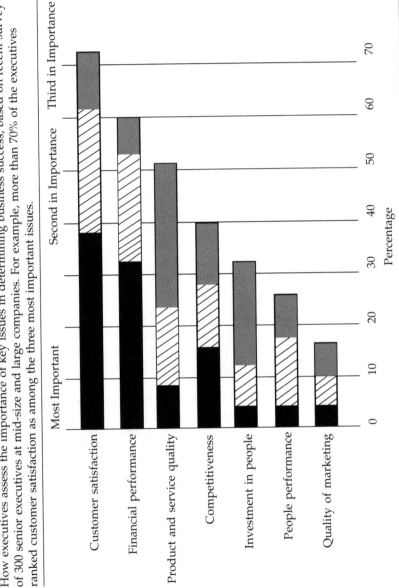

Exhibit 6–2 A Matter of Priorities.

Source: Towers Perrin, "A Matter of Priorities." *The New York Times*, February 19, 1995, p. 23.

nately, human nature being what it is brings out the worst in many managers, particularly those who are unsure of themselves. Such managers are apt to be autocratic and controlling. Tom Melohn, in his book *The New Partnership* (Vermont: Oliver Wright, 1994), describes the twelve-year transformation he experienced with North American Tool and Die. Throughout, Melohn describes the characteristics of the new partnership that enabled him to turn around his company:

- Honesty
- Trust
- "Do unto others as you would have them do unto you"
- Teamwork
- Finding, hiring, motivating, and keeping super employees
- Releasing employee creativity
- Saying "thank you"
- Small—beautiful and more fun
- Responsibility and competence
- Heart and quality
- Service, not abject servitude
- Helping yourself by helping others
- Enthusiasm and humor
- Leadership

Melohn's premise about the importance of people is profound. Remember what we said earlier in this book: Typically 6% to 10% of most manufacturing firms' budgets represent the compensation costs for people. In the nonprofit, this figure is in the 70% to 80% range. What then are the implications of allowing the human spirit to thrive in a nonprofit? The implications are great. Just think how much more productive our volunteers and staff can be in delivering core mission programs if their leadership embraces Melohn's philosophy: "If you reach out and care—genuinely care—for your fellow employee, there's no limit to what you can achieve. . . . Just go do it! For your sake . . . for your kids . . . for their kids . . ." (p. 248). Melohn is right. Let us have the courage to reengineer our nonprofit's attitude toward the volunteer and the staff. The irony is our service-based missions compel us to make the workplace more humane and conducive to productivity. We must have the fortitude and confidence to execute.

THE CURRENT HUMAN RESOURCES PARADIGM

Typically, nonprofits have organized the delivery of human resources in three different locations on the organizational chart: (1) The needs of the board, the chair, and individual directors are typically addressed in the office of the executive director; (2) volunteers are served through either volunteer services or chapter or field services; and (3) staff are served through a personnel or human resources office.

The configuration serving the board and the directors is a natural outgrowth of the partnership that the chief executive must develop and perpetuate with the chair and the board as a whole. Typically, the executive director works as the staff person to organize and deliver governing board workshops that provide a venue for board training. In addition, the executive director works with the chair of the nominating or board development committee to put together board orientation materials and to conduct board orientation programs for new and continuing board members. The executive director's office also maintains board minutes and the personnel files of all board members.

The configuration of a volunteer services or field/chapter unit parallels the historical need of national offices to recreate/replicate their structures and service delivery mechanisms in local affiliates. In addition to providing programmatic support, these organizational units are typically charged with maintaining and updating volunteer (personnel) files, providing technical training and volunteer development courses, and providing volunteers with counsel and support as individuals engaged in service delivery. Often, such organizational units provide key volunteer leaders with staff assistance in carrying out their local or affiliate board and advisory committee assignments.

Unfortunately, the configuration for staff is typically limited, albeit archaic in most nonprofits. For example, many of the personnel offices of large and small nonprofits had their genesis with the administrative assistant or secretary in the executive director's office. All too frequently, the personnel function was narrowly conceived as payroll and benefits processing, and a secretary or administrative assistant was assigned the task. In many cases, such a function was perceived as a necessary administrative task. It is only in recent memory that the concept of human resources in its broadest and most developmental of definitions has begun to emerge in the nonprofit. Even at that, however, the sector is not routinely peopled with enlightened human resource directors who embrace the notion that the key to successful reengineering is an empowered volunteer and staff workforce.

Now more than ever, the sector requires enlightened human resources

managers who comprehend that the human resources department must
do the following:

- Play an increased role in the organization with a small yet dedicated cadre of human resources specialists who have the respect of
  volunteers and staff alike.
- Put increased emphasis on employee selection and development.
- Serve as facilitator of training, either through its own staff or with
  the assistance of outside expertise.
- Decrease the focus on wage, job classification, and employee relations and assess the practicality of contracting out such services
  rather than providing them in-house.
- Redefine current classification systems to mirror and reinforce the
  operating environment that the executive director and the board
  want to create as the result of reengineering.

People are the ones who make the words of their nonprofit's mission
come to life, therefore, the nonprofit must develop a new human
resources model that embraces the attributes just enumerated. Such a
model needs to recognize the fundamental training and developmental
needs of all persons associated with the charity—be they board, volunteers, or staff—and celebrate and reward the contributions of all who
serve. The next section of this chapter talks about the human resources
needs of the nonprofit of the future and how to reconfigure the way in
which we currently support our nonprofit's most important resources:
the board, volunteers, and staff.

REENGINEERING VOLUNTEER
AND STAFF RESOURCES

Currently, neither the for-profit nor the nonprofit sector is poised for
tomorrow's jobs. This is especially true of the nonprofit—it has begun to
tackle organization-wide reengineering only in the last few years.
Reengineering radically changes the way in which nonprofits do their
work. As a result, everything that employees and volunteers do, as well
as how they do it, needs to be scrutinized.

Many director-level and associate- and assistant vice president–level
positions are likely to disappear with reengineering. These middle and
upper-level management positions will be replaced by people who serve
on the front line, answering questions and providing information to the

nonprofit's constituency. These frontline people will be responsible for the continuous redesign and improvement of administrative processes and program and service delivery. As the nonprofit's lifeline, these essential staff and volunteers will require continuous coaching from other staff and volunteers who are particularly skilled in teaching people how to provide services and who have hands-on service delivery experience. These are not the people who have traditionally sat in a personnel or a human resources office and have sporadically supplied skills training programs. Rather, these are the folks who, because of their firsthand experience in doing the job, can coach individuals and teams alike on how to get the job done more productively and at higher service levels so that the scarce resources of the nonprofit are visibly focused on the mission-based activities and services rather than on ancillary administrative support services. The social worker who trains volunteers to handle crisis calls from homeless teenagers or battered women is one example. Docent training provided by senior docents to new docents at the Bruce Museum is yet another example.

The capstone in this new organizational model that empowers the human spirit is the staff–volunteer partnership at the most senior level (the executive director and the board chair) as motivator, organization-wide decision maker, and instiller of followership. Ronald Heifetz describes the requisites for leadership in a rapidly changing world in his book *Leadership Without Easy Answers* (Cambridge, MA: Harvard University Press, 1994). The leader

- Is an individual who is able to identify challenges—those gaps between aspiration and reality—and focus people's attention on those challenges. Such a leader needs to be able to articulate her/his vision and be passionate about its importance to the organization.
- Regulates the level of distress through confrontation of the issues and keeps pace with the rate of change. The leader monitors how much pain and discomfort people can take and carefully and decisively comes to closure on outstanding issues.
- Keeps focused on relevant issues. The leader is not sucked into the vortex of issues that are clearly not relevant to her/his organization.
- Has poise and inner discipline. A leader manifests this self-confidence in such a way as to instill trust and, consequently, followership among constituents.

Further, in our view, being a leader means identifying the skills (training) and the knowledge (development and education) staff and volunteers need to become masters or to become the very finest at what they do.

What does this mean for the nonprofit sector? Simply put, it means that those of us in the sector need to carefully orchestrate how we balance the need for delivering core mission activities, increasing productivity, and enhancing service levels or the quality of our programs to the constituents we serve. Can we do it in the way in which we have historically recruited, trained, evaluated, recognized, rewarded, clustered, compensated, and titled people? We think not. In fact, we believe that three ingredients are necessary to make reengineering successful:

1. Fundamental change in human resources management.
2. Changes in human resources policies and procedures that are in concert with administrative and program/service process changes.
3. Recognition that staff and volunteer efforts need to be intertwined and that individuals as well as teams must be viewed within the context of the broader mission and vision of the charity.

Richard J. Schonberger, in "Human Resource Management Lessons from a Decade of Total Quality Management and Reengineering," in the Summer 1994 edition of the *California Management Review*, talks about shifting human resources premises and practices:

- *Jobs*:   Process improvement is critical and should be part of everyone's job. Process improvement should no longer be left to managers and specialists. Process improvement needs to come from those most intimately knowledgeable about the process, no matter what their job.

- *Teams*:   Multifunctional work-flow teams or cross-functional work groups whose membership embraces users as well as initiators are critical to process reengineering. The chances for success are greater among teams than lone rangers.

- *Titles*:   Staff are associates, not workers. It is critical to reinforce the philosophy of teamwork and empowerment. The use of language is essential to reinforcing a change in behavior and how the human spirit is managed to create a productive environment.

- *Managers*:   Everyone—not just supervisory people—is a manager. That is, everyone shares in the process of managing change, managing a program, providing a service. Former managers become facilitators. Facilitators ensure that the work of teams is focused and productive.

- *Leadership*: Inspirational leaders are rare. Our society cannot depend on their appearance. Cooperation, shaped by the concepts of continuous quality improvement, ensures leadership throughout the organization.

What implications does this change in human resources premises and practices have as we begin to reengineer the volunteer and staff resources of our nonprofit?

- Everyone's job—volunteer and staff alike—must include process improvement, be it in administrative activities or program and service delivery.
- We must think of our nonprofit's mission and overall vision as serving as the locus for the creation of multifunctional as opposed to single-focus work teams. Such work teams will tackle a specific process assignment and disband. (This represents a radical departure from the standing committee-driven operating culture that typifies the nonprofit sector.)
- We must consider giving up titles such as administrative assistants and secretaries and call such front-line employees "associates" and "client service representatives."
- Staff professionals, middle-level managers, and their related staff emerge as "coaches" and "facilitators," blurring the distinction between line and staff.
- Starting from the top of the organization and moving throughout, people must be willing to share knowledge; communicate on an even plane; and demonstrate common sense, empathy, trust, and kindness. This sharing of knowledge needs to be intentional. It cannot be borne solely of good intentions, as good intentions are often haphazard at best.

What does this mean for the performance, recognition, reinforcement, and the pay and reward practices of our nonprofits? It means radical redesign.

In the new human resources–focused paradigm just described, executive directors and boards will have to ensure that

- Nonprofits hold teams and individuals alike accountable not only for the processes they redesign but for actively tracking their individual and team improvements and communicating them with the constituents they serve.

- Reward systems for staff and volunteers are redesigned in such a way as to rely on measurable, quality-oriented results, rather than solely on the subjective judgments of managers and supervisors.
- Special recognition is provided in a systematic, rather than on a sporadic basis, and in a public way at awards ceremonies, in staff and volunteer publications, and at chapter and board meetings.
- The charity goes out of its way to recognize team rather than individual performance in a predetermined manner.
- Behavior is modified to produce positive results. Therefore, coaches and leaders will have to be careful about their choice of words. For example, instead of "error" or "mistake," coaches and leaders will have to learn such language as "challenge," "problem," and "mishap." These terms will encourage team members to be more forthright and to strive to eradicate the root cause of the problem without fear of retribution.
- Performance evaluation will become multidimensional, that is, up and down as well as across the organizational structure and including constituents who are served. Such evaluation should also include volunteers as well as staff.
- Nonmonetary rewards include training and development, working in teams, working closely with volunteers and constituents, participating in strategic planning and resource allocation processes, going on field trips to see what other nonprofits are doing and attending professional meetings, making presentations at board meetings, and the like.

How does such radical redesign get implemented? One of the most powerful ways is through the reengineering of current compensation systems that are based on hierarchical, rather than on team-oriented or flattened organizational structures.

DESIGNING COMPENSATION SYSTEMS TO SUPPORT THE REDESIGNED CHARITY

Almost all nonprofit managers are wedded to a pay grade and classification structure that was developed during the industrialized era when job hierarchy and specialization were highly valued. Such pay grade and classification structures are designed to fit a vertical organizational structure and culture. As organizational structures, processes, policies, and procedures are reengineered, there is wisdom in opting for fewer pay grades for all types of jobs and more lateral movement; the latter supports the flattening brought about by the reengineering. These radical departures from the hierarchical bureaucracy necessitate radical approaches to pay. Banding is one response.

A *banded* classification and pay structure has radically fewer vertical levels and job titles and wider salary boundaries. As a consequence, banding is a flatter and broader pay structure. Peter LeBlanc, a certified compensation professional, describes the four key design features of banding in his article "Banding—The New Pay Structure for the Transformed Organization" (in *Perspectives in Total Compensation*, March 1992, published by the American Compensation Association):

- Fewer grade levels (bands) and titles
- Alternative career tracks
- Wider salary ranges with no midpoints
- Two or more market-based pay ranges per band

As these major features are so different from the classic compensation systems, banding also requires that the pay delivery, job evaluation, and market-pricing techniques be reassessed. Banding is an emerging system, and LeBlanc is quick to point out there is no ideal number of bands to fit all organizations. In developing the vertical structure of the band, the most challenging task is defining the lines of distinction between each contributor band. This is especially important when this system becomes the basis for promotion and internal equity. In this approach, jobs are assigned to a band on the basis of internal job evaluation factors and to a pay range on the basis of external labor market factors.

Exhibit 6–3, taken from LeBlanc's article, illustrates a thirteen-band structure, starting at the nonexempt entry level, Clerical Support, Associate, and through to the position of President. There are seven managerial and individual contributor bands that are parallel dual-career bands, leaving only two conventional job family ladder steps (band 5, Specialist, and band 6, Senior Specialist). The dual-career track begins with the first level of management, band 7, and ends at band 11.

The case study on page 136, taken from LeBlanc's article, provides a real example of one of our first attempts to adapt banding to a university setting. Only the name of the university has been edited from our final analysis.

CASE STUDY

Establishing Broad Bands, Salary Ranges, and Pay Zones

The new compensation program recommended for the university is designed with five broad bands or levels that encompass all positions and incorporate the concept of broad salary ranges for each band and shorter within-band pay range zones.

Each of the five bands includes a variety of jobs with differing levels of appropriate compensation. Because of the small number of bands and the wide range of salaries associated with the jobs in each, it is advisable, at least for some bands, to further subdivide the salary ranges into pay range zones, each representing one half or one third of the salary range. In some cases, the pay range zones will accommodate entry-level and intermediate-level workers in the same job or job family (e.g., receptionists and administrative assistants, or custodial and maintenance). In other cases, the different zones will accommodate different types of jobs that have different market positions (e.g., assistant dean of students and bursar). The compensation philosophy of the university should guide the relationship of the salary ranges and pay range zones to the market.

The slotting of jobs into bands should be based on the criteria developed specifically for this purpose. Because market survey data are neither available nor necessary for every job in the university, the salary ranges should be based on available market data. Placement within pay range zones should be based on a combination of available market data and internal comparisons/relationships.

All salaries in each band must be within the parameters of the respective salary ranges. For this reason, the university, for now, will need to establish salary ranges based on current salaries, with a goal of changing the salary band parameters as funds become available to address salary inequities, both internal and external. Presented below are three sets of salary bands/pay range zones. First are the recommended salary bands and pay range zones for the current situation. We then present recommended salary bands/pay range zones that may be adopted during the transition (while some improvements are made). Finally, we present the salary bands/pay range zones that would be appropriate were the university's salaries currently competitive.

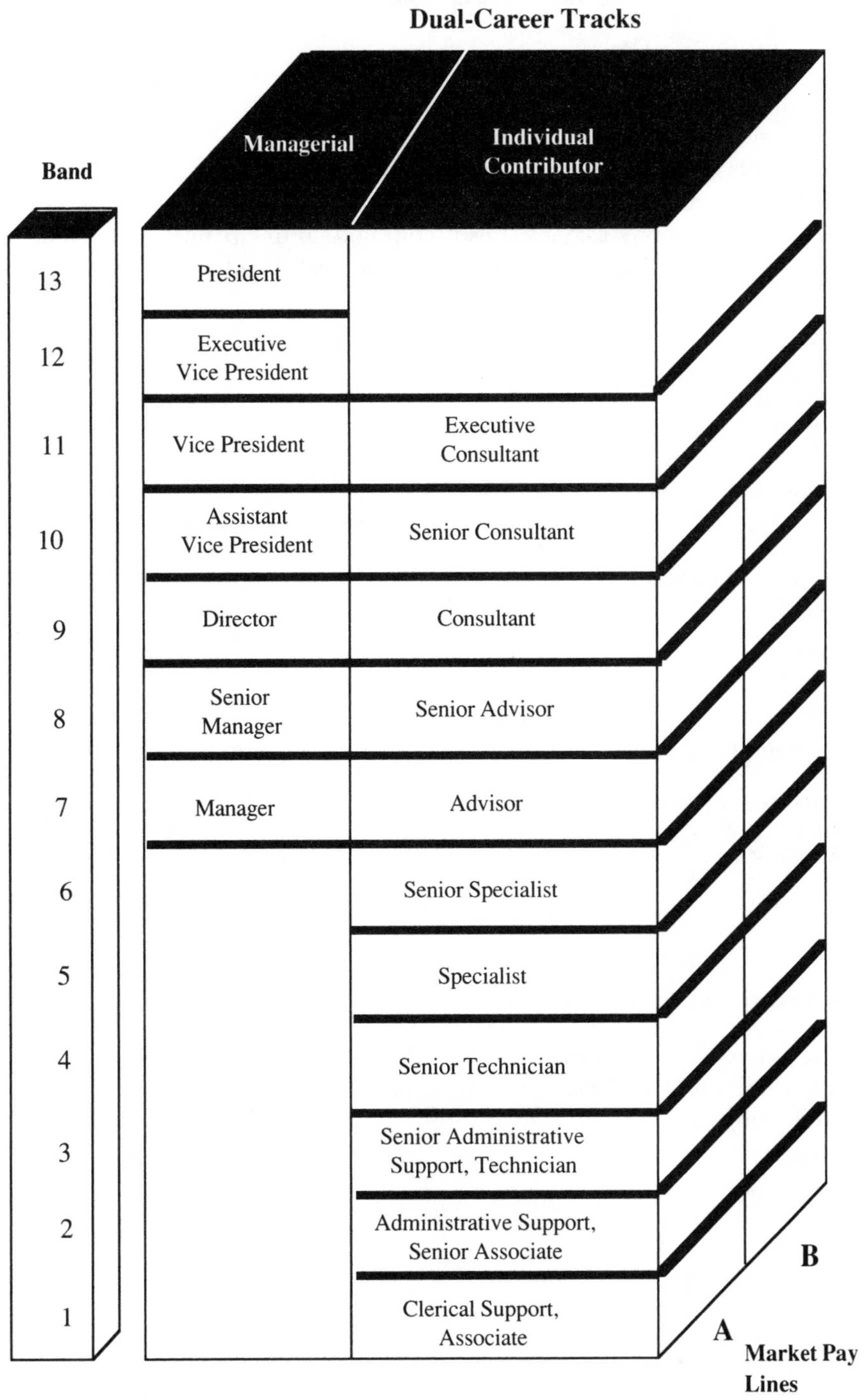

Dual-Career Tracks

Band	Managerial	Individual Contributor
13	President	
12	Executive Vice President	
11	Vice President	Executive Consultant
10	Assistant Vice President	Senior Consultant
9	Director	Consultant
8	Senior Manager	Senior Advisor
7	Manager	Advisor
6		Senior Specialist
5		Specialist
4		Senior Technician
3		Senior Administrative Support, Technician
2		Administrative Support, Senior Associate
1		Clerical Support, Associate

A   B   Market Pay Lines

Exhibit 6–3   Establishing Broad Bands.

Salary Ranges/Pay Range Zones for Now

The current situation finds the university with outlier salaries at both the low and the high end of almost every band. The following salary ranges/pay range zones accommodate this reality.

The lowest and highest current salaries in each band are as follows:

Executive	$55.4–$76.7	(Leader)
Manager/Senior Professional	30.8–65.5	(Coach/Facilitator)
Administrative/Senior Professional	14.6–46.5	(Coach/Facilitator)
Administrative Support	10.7–26.8	(Frontline Associates)
Service	11.4–26.7	(Frontline Associates)

The following ranges simply round down for minimums and up for maximums.

Band	Minimum	Maximum
Executive	$55.0	$77.0
Manager/Professional	$30.0	$66.0
Administrative/Senior Professional	$14.0	$47.0
Administrative Support	$10.0	$27.0
Service	$11.0	$27.0

The Next Step: During the Transition

As the university overcomes some of the more significant lags in compensation and addresses the more serious internal inequities, the following ranges would be appropriate:

Band	Minimum	Maximum
Executive	$55.0	$80.0
Manager/Professional	$35.0	$65.0
Administrative/Senior Professional	$20.0	$50.0
Administrative Support	$13.0	$35.0
Service	$12.0	$30.0

Reaching the Goal of Parity

Were the university able to reach the goal of market parity today, the following illustrates what our recommended salary ranges and pay range zones would be. Using this model, pay range zones can be added to the above salary range, as appropriate.

We offer two examples. Each has salary ranges 100% long, with overlaps from 10% to 20%.

The first example has a single salary range for the Executive band, two pay range zones each for the Manager/Senior Professional and Administrative/Senior Professional levels, and three pay range zones each for the Administrative Support and Service levels:

Band

Executive
|—————————————————————————————————————|
$50.0 $100.0

Manager/Senior
Professional
|————— Zone 1 —————|————— Zone 2 —————|
$35.0 $52.5 $70.0

Administrative/
Senior Professional
|————— Zone 1 —————|————— Zone 2 —————|
$25.0 $37.5 $50.0

Administrative
Support
|—— Zone 1 ——|—— Zone 2 ——|—— Zone 3 ——|
$20.0 $26.0 $32.0 $40.0

Service
|—— Zone 1 ——|—— Zone 2 ——|—— Zone 3 ——|
$15.0 $20.0 $25.0 $30.0

The second example has two pay zones each for the Executive and Manager/Senior Professional levels, and three pay range zones each for the Administrative/Senior Professional, Administrative Support, and Service levels:

Band

Executive
|————— Zone 1 —————|————— Zone 2 —————|
$50.0 $75.5 $100.0

Manager/Senior
Professional
|————— Zone 1 —————|————— Zone 2 —————|
$35.0 $52.5 $70.0

Administrative/
Senior Professional
|—— Zone 1 ——|—— Zone 2 ——|—— Zone 3 ——|
$25.0 $33.5 $41.5 $50.0

Administrative
Support
|—— Zone 1 ——|—— Zone 2 ——|—— Zone 3 ——|
$20.0 $26.0 $32.0 $40.0

Service
|—— Zone 1 ——|—— Zone 2 ——|—— Zone 3 ——|
$15.0 $20.0 $25.0 $30.0

Finally, using the second example, we show how positions would be slotted to these salary ranges and pay zones:

Band

Executive

Zone 1	Zone 2
$50.0	$75.5	$100.0
P, other senior staff	Provost, VP[1]	

Manager/Senior
Executive

Zone 1	Zone 2
$35.0	$52.5	$70.0
Dean of Students	Director of Libraries	

Administrative/
Senior Professional

Zone 1	Zone 2	Zone 3
$25.0	$33.5	$41.5	$50.0
Admissions Counselor	Director Annual Fund	Director Planned Giving	

Administrative
Support

Zone 1	Zone 2	Zone 3
$20.0	$26.0	$32.0	$40.0
Secretary	Office Manager	Personnel Assistant	

Service

Zone 1	Zone 2	Zone 3
$15.0	$20.0	$25.0	$30.0
Custodian	Carpenter	Security Lieutenant	

Conclusion

Over time, as the university conducts salary surveys, the number and type of jobs surveyed may be expanded and refined to permit more accurate setting of salary ranges/pay range bands.

In addition, the university may wish to request a more tailored cut of data from the College and University Personnel Association in order to ascertain salaries in comparable colleges and universities, rather than relying primarily on national data.

We recommend that the university begin by adopting only one salary range for the Executive band, two pay range zones each for the Manager/Senior Professional and Administrative/Senior Professional bands, and three pay range zones each for the Administrative Support and Service bands.

---

[1]Some VP positions will fall in Zone 1, some in Zone 2. It would also be reasonable to slot some senior staff positions to each level, depending on market data.

REENGINEERING PERFORMANCE MEASUREMENT FOR BOARD, VOLUNTEERS, AND STAFF

Equally as critical as the reengineering of compensation and pay structures is the redesign of performance measurement systems for staff, the executive director, volunteers, the board chair, and the board. In such redesign, the following elements must be included:

- Feedback from leaders, coaches/facilitators, and frontline associates, as well as constituents and volunteers
- Focus on the commitment to the nonprofit's mission and vision
- Commitment to constituent, volunteer, and staff service
- Capacity to continuously improve administrative activities, processes, and program and service delivery
- Measurable performance standards linked to broad strategic goals, specific programmatic objectives, team/group objectives, and so on
- Commitment to communicating knowledge to team members and serving as educator, facilitator, and coach

The reengineering of performance management systems for board, volunteers, and staff requires considerable time and input from across the organization. Using the elements just enumerated, we recommend that you engage in a series of discussions with cross-functional teams to determine how these elements can be translated specifically to address your nonprofit. For example, how do you measure how effectively a social worker or volunteer has responded to juveniles in crisis on your hot line? Do we use the same criteria for the volunteer and the staff member or should they be different? How do we measure the quality of the hot line service that is provided by a team comprised of volunteers and staff?

Such is the detail that needs to be developed for every element of the performance management survey. Do not, however, get overly enthusiastic. Focus on the key elements that will ensure that your volunteer and staff resources are being applied in the most productive manner possible. Also ask yourself how to not only create but imbue your organization with the spirit inherent in the Chinese proverb quoted at the beginning of this chapter: "Of the best leader, when he is gone, they will say: We did it ourselves."

CREATING A NEW VOLUNTEER–STAFF PARTNERSHIP

As your nonprofit reengineers the way in which volunteers and staff work together to support core mission activities, remember to

- Avoid the urge to prepare the ideal human organization. Specifically, avoid kicking off the change process with employee satisfaction surveys; team building; training in conflict resolution, stress reduction, leadership, communication, and listening skills; or alterations to the compensation package. All of these are valuable but will surely lead nowhere if not connected to a fundamental understanding on the part of volunteer and staff of the mission, vision, and constituency needs of your nonprofit.
- Cross-train frontline associates and facilitators/coaches and get to know where all aspects of work are done.
- Rely on multifunctional teams and work groups and constantly reinforce the need to break down organizational walls and geographical boundaries (for example, those between the national office and local chapters and affiliates) and address the needs of multiple constituents.
- As challenging as it may be, as frontliners slowly, yet progressively, take ownership of process, service, and program delivery improvement, cease and desist from the corporate lingo of "errors" and "mistakes" and move toward positive language that describes "challenges" and "mishaps."
- Embrace performance management systems that include the input of multiple constituents.
- Put the idea of work-family needs first, recognizing that solving soft, people issues goes a long way toward increasing quality and output.

What better way to end this chapter on reengineering volunteer and staff resources than a case study that provides fascinating insight into how to increase productivity while improving the quality of people's lives?

CASE STUDY

Reengineering with a Work-Family Lens

Looking at reengineering through a work-family perspective can shatter barriers to change. In the March 1, 1995, *Wall Street Journal* (p. B1), Lotte Bailyn, a management professor at Massachusetts

Institute of Technology, put it succinctly: "If you say you want people to be more productive, they fear they will be laid off or given much more work. But if you say up front, 'We're working on a double agenda' of improving productivity and the quality of worker's lives, people bring more energy and creativity to restructuring work."

At a Xerox unit, managers had found it difficult to get salespeople and customer-service people to cooperate. But when employees and Dr. Bailyn's researchers sat down to discuss improving people's work-life balance, the same idea—getting sales and customer-service people to work together—was embraced by the two groups, who soon began to work more cooperatively. "We engaged these people because they felt there was something there for them personally. That's what created the energy," Dr. Bailyn says.

Few companies are thinking about work-family programs this way. But more are paying the price of taking the opposite track—focusing only on the technical dimensions of reengineering. Employers not only intensify stress and damage morale, but also "create a vicious cycle that undermines family and community." Ultimately, she adds, that hurts present and future employees—and defeats "what companies are trying to do in the first place."

Isn't it time that the nonprofit rigorously examines the ways in which people—board, volunteers, and staff—are treated? We think so and we believe that such a humanistic perspective would go a long way toward improving nonprofit productivity and mission-based outcomes.

CHAPTER SEVEN

Reengineering Relationships: Mergers, Partnerships, and Strategic Alliances

In the 1960s, the economy was soaring. Nonprofits were in their financial and programmatic heyday, growing exponentially and without any real concern for what challenges the future might bring. The corporate sector was booming as well. Conglomerates began acquiring companies with an almost seeming vengeance. At that time, the corporate mentality was "bigger is better." There was the conviction that synergy would result in the equation: $1 + 1 = 3$.

The ensuing reality has been painful for both sectors. For the nonprofit, expansion for expansion's sake has meant a burgeoning of organizations with mission statements and programs and services that sound the proverbial "all things to all people." Indeed, it has become difficult to discern what differentiates one nonprofit from the next, leaving funders, clients, and other constituents in a quandary about where to go for their particular program and service needs. Competition has become fierce. Nonprofits are looking, more than ever, to reengineer relationships with their competitors through mergers, the formation of strategic alliances, and the creation of partnerships. In some cases, the nonprofit world has begun to create separate for-profit entities to generate revenues, so that their nonprofit status is not jeopardized.

For the corporate world, it has become a time of continued downsizing, renewed focus on profitability and the bottom line, and the bitter remembrances of the mergers and acquisitions spawn of the 1960s. Philip Mirvis, a former professor of business administration at Boston University, reports in *Building the Competitive Workforce: Investing in*

Human Capital for Success (New York: Wiley, 1993) that 50% of corporate mergers have failed to deliver premerger expectations. Mirvis cites the Shearson acquisition of the Lehman Brothers investment bank as an example of the purchase of a proven franchise that became crippled during the merger process. Relations between the senior leadership of the two merged companies grew acrimonious, and embittered Lehman executives resigned.

Indeed, such negative experiences are rather commonplace in the for-profit sector. Nevertheless, positive examples of mergers, partnerships, and strategic alliances abound as well—the corporate world has been reengineering relationships for a long time with an eye toward increased profitability. What can the astute nonprofit executive director and board learn from the for-profit world? Much. The nonprofit manager and volunteer can learn what works and what typically does not work. In fact, there are steadily growing numbers of reengineered relationships in the nonprofit sector. In this chapter, we first define merger, partnership, and strategic alliance. We then talk about mergers in the nonprofit world and what it takes to make them work. We address this sector's current challenge of learning how to share rather than compete and deciding which programs and services are core to the mission, as opposed to those that are supporting, as well as non–mission-based activities that may more appropriately be provided by outside agencies expert in their delivery (e.g., accounting, payroll, information technology).

Defining the Terminology

Webster's dictionary provides the most succinct definitions of merger and partnership.

Merger. The absorption of an estate, a contract, or an interest in another; absorption by a corporation of one or more others; also: any of various methods of combining two or more organizations (as business concerns).

Partnership. The state of being a partner: participation. A legal relation existing between two or more persons contractually associated as joint principals in a business; close cooperation between parties having specified and joint rights and responsibilities.

In the case of a merger, the two or more parties are combined into one new operating entity. The new entity redefines or creates a new mission statement, a strategic and resource allocation plan, and an operating plan. In most cases, the merger is not of equal parties in terms of the size of the operating budget, number of staff members, or available operating reserves. In many cases, one entity is expected to give up a considerable amount of the autonomy it had as an independently functioning entity. Under most circumstances, a merger is associated with staff and volunteer angst, as both parties must and are expected to compromise at various points along the way.

Partnerships, on the other hand, are initiated by willing parties who are set on a course of close cooperation, as well as joint risk and reward. This is not to suggest that all mergers are akin to hostile takeovers or unfriendly acquisitions. In such a case, each party brings something different but complementary to the other partners or brings some asset the other partners want or believe they need to be successful. Indeed, many mergers in the nonprofit sector are of willing parties. However, in a partnership, there are really no winners or losers at the front end of the negotiation. (Remember that partners can be bought out or eased out by their partnership agreements if they do not deliver their fair share.) There are simply those with more influence (in the case of a for-profit partnership, this is evident in the number of shares or units held by an individual partner), better market position, or more political clout. Although there is obvious jockeying at the formation of a partnership, it is bereft of the kind of disruption and anxiety that characterizes a merger. A merger is typified by force and the conquering hero mentality. A partnership is typified by the Quaker concept of equals as well as team spirit.

As you might guess, the term *strategic alliance* is not in the dictionary. This is due in large measure to the relative newness of this concept and approach. We have, therefore, provided the standard definitions of strategic and alliance.

Strategic Alliance. (strategic) necessary to or important in the initiation, conduct, or completion of a strategic plan: of great importance within an integrated whole or to a planned effect; (alliance) an association to further the common interests of the members; union by relationship in qualities: a treaty of alliance.

A *strategic alliance*, then, is the intentional relationship of one entity with another to accomplish joint objectives, deliver projects and programs of common interest and/or work from a position of greater market strength and quality for a given period of time. A strategic alliance is profoundly dependent on good will and on the individual and the unique strengths of each entity. Strategic alliances are, in many ways, bound by their particular market demand and niche; they depend, to a large extent, on changing market forces as well as on the volunteers and staff who manage and lead the entities.

MERGER: DOES IT WORK IN THE NONPROFIT WORLD?

In our view, mergers can work in the nonprofit sector. However, if asked to provide success stories, we would have a difficult time reeling off a list of names across the sector. Perhaps the most common, successful examples are in education at the K–12 level and the post–secondary level and in health care. Examples include the merger of a boy's prep school and a girl's boarding school, the merger of a men's college and a women's college, or the merger of two hospitals in the same geographic catchment area.

Examples in other segments of the nonprofit sector are not as abundant. This, we believe, is due in large measure to the mission, vision, goals, and objectives of such organizations and the passionately held view of boards and executive directors alike that their organization is somehow different, special, or unique. This is not to suggest, however, that merger is an anathema in the sector. In fact, growing numbers of organizations with similar missions and constituencies are merging.

We think that the case study below provides the elements for a successful merger. As you read the text following the case study, you will soon understand why we think this merger will succeed when so many others have failed.

CASE STUDY

Merger of Family Services Nonprofit and City Agency

On March 31, 1995, after a year of planning, the Family Center Inc. of Greenwich, Connecticut, and Family and Children's Services Inc. of Stamford, Connecticut, announced their merger as Family Centers Inc.

Family and Children's Services sought the merger in 1994 after its administrative staff and directors realized that ongoing losses in governmental and nonprofit grant funding would impede the agency's ability to maintain its service delivery levels. The Family Center, Greenwich's oldest human services agency, traces its legacy to the 1895 founding of the Greenwich Aid Society, which eventually became the United Workers of Greenwich. A series of mergers of social welfare agencies in the 1930s gave birth to the Greenwich Center for Child and Family Services, later renamed the Family Center.

The Family Center had a budget of $2.4 million and offered counseling, educational, support, and consulting services to strengthen family life. Family and Children's Services, founded in the early 1890s, had an annual budget of $1 million. It offered services similar to those enumerated for the Family Center in Stamford, Darien, and New Canaan, Connecticut.

In an interview with the *Greenwich Times* (April 1, 1995), the president of the new entity said:

> The merger will strengthen services. . . . It will put the newly constituted agency in line for more government and local charitable funding because it now will serve an entire region. Today is a very important day because I think . . . we've been compartmentalized a long time and behaved in many ways as if problems stopped at the town line. But in reality we have a lot of problems and program needs that exist from town to town to town.

The merged agency will retain the combined staff of the two former agencies, totaling slightly more than 100 full and part-time workers. Whether additional employees are hired will depend on future funding obtained by Family Centers Inc. (the new agency). Interestingly, although some financial and administrative functions of the merged agency will be housed together, many programs and services will remain decentralized to provide maximum coverage across the four Connecticut municipalities involved. New administrative titles, with top officials of the former Greenwich agency filling many of the top slots of the newly combined agency, have been created.

When queried about the reaction of the staff of the two former agencies to the announced merger, the new president commented: "We've been working on combining the two agencies all along, so now the announcement of the merger, in some ways for our staff, is anticlimactic."

Before engaging in any serious thought about a merger, consider the following:

- Too often, nonprofits consider merger as a means of dealing with sustained operating deficits or immediate cash flow problems, without thinking about the longer term consequences.

- Frequently, when the complex process of merger is done out of desperation, there are compromised financial gains, if not total failure.
- No matter how compatible the missions and constituents of the two nonprofits appear, *how* a merger is implemented (as opposed to the perceived strategic fit) determines whether the merger will be a success or a failure.

Mergers need necessarily to emerge as an offensive rather than a defensive posture and with certain, achievable goals in mind. Such goals should include (1) enhancing the delivery of a particular service or program, (2) enhancing the nonprofit's competitive position in the marketplace, (3) pooling financial resources, and (4) exploiting critical mass or advantages of scale. If, in fact, potential merger candidates do not believe that merger can achieve such desired goals, they should cease such exploration. If, however, the two charities believe that the desired goals could be realized through a merger, they should undertake the three-tier assessment outlined in Exhibit 7–1.

LESSONS TO BE LEARNED FROM YOUR COLLEAGUES

With respect to merger with another nonprofit, remember that

- Productivity will initially decrease rather than increase, as the time expended by both volunteers and staff will be disrupted as new processes, procedures, and policies are implemented.
- It is critical to talk openly about how volunteers and employees feel about the merger.
- If people have no sense of ownership in the new schema, individuals as well as departments will begin to feel alone or forgotten. From the beginning, take steps to ensure that both volunteers and staff will have a sense of ownership.
- It is important to recognize, if not celebrate, the integrity of programs that maintain their own identity within the merged charity.
- The new entity must be intentional about developing the values, norms, and new traditions that will sustain it. This is the ultimate labor of love that must be exercised by volunteers and staff alike.
- Senior leadership should act definitively yet allow enough time in the merger process to address the people and cultural issues previously enumerated.

Strategic Level: Organizational Compatibility Criteria

❏ Mission and vision
❏ Organizational culture (board, staff, and volunteers)
❏ Organizational structure
❏ Governance
❏ Identity and image within the nonprofit sector
❏ Programs and services
❏ Fund-raising history and capacity
❏ Facilities and tangible assets
❏ Overall financial condition
❏ Geographical proximity
❏ Technology and related support systems
❏ Constituent support
❏ Strong chief executive and board sponsorship
❏ Capacity to counteract opposing forces and organizations
❏ Realistic understanding of the costs (human, financial, and physical) of merger
❏ Realistic expectations

Operating Level: Due Diligence Compatibility Criteria

❏ Ten years of financial trendline data, comparing actual with budget
❏ Accounting policies
❏ Cost allocation methodologies
❏ Internal controls environment
❏ Consistency of financial management and reporting
❏ Auditor's work papers
❏ Employee benefits packages (health and life insurance, retirement)
❏ Terms and conditions of employment
❏ Terms and conditions for volunteer involvement
❏ Compensation packages for senior staff
❏ Compensation and performance appraisal systems for staff
❏ Banking relationships (cash available, outstanding indebtedness, debt covenants)
❏ Asset conditions (endowment, funds functioning as endowment, physical plant, and equipment)
❏ Outstanding and significant commitments and contingent liabilities (e.g. pending litigation, self-insurance, incentive compensation, lease, or other commitments)

Human Resource Level: Staff and Volunteer Compatibility Criteria

❏ Promotion, transfer, layoff policies
❏ Unionization of employees
❏ Type of severance arrangements
❏ Outplacement resources
❏ Volunteer and staff retraining and development
❏ Relocation expenses
❏ Morale of volunteers and staff

Exhibit 7–1   "Go–No Go" Merger Criteria Checklist
Source: ©Pappas Consulting Group Inc.

- Senior- and middle-level staff are most vulnerable to reductions in force and not all board members will be nominated to serve on the board of the merged entity.

- Senior- and middle-level staff should take advantage of the transition associated with the implementation of the merger by defining new ways of doing work at your nonprofit.

- Senior- and middle-level staff should positively exploit this time of change by providing employees an opportunity to work in new cross-functional teams to redesign processes, policies, procedures, programs, and services as appropriate.

- The merger process is extraordinarily complex and requires strong leadership and sponsorship at the board and executive director levels of both entities.

PARTNERSHIPS: LEARNING TO SHARE RATHER THAN COMPETE

Previously, we defined partnership as a legal or contractual relationship between two or more parties having designated single and joint rights and responsibilities. In the world of nonprofits, partnerships sometimes are spelled out in written legal documents, but other times they are more informal, cooperative relationships. Whatever form they take, partnerships must be clearly defined. Both parties must ask and answer several fundamental questions:

- What is to be ventured; what is to be gained from the relationship?
- To whose benefit is the anticipated outcome (fund-raising effort, public service announcement, new program or service)?
- For what period of time is the partnership binding? For one particular fund-raising event? For a series of events? For a period of years?

The Los Angeles office of the U.S. Committee for UNICEF is a case in point.

CASE STUDY

The Time Has Come for Community and Corporate Partnerships

The combined 1994–1995 annual report and 1995–1996 budget request of the Los Angeles office of the U.S. Committee for

UNICEF are clear about the way the organization is reengineering its relationships with other nonprofits and the corporate and foundation community:

- As Angelenos deal with the recovery from the natural and human-made disasters of recent years, the appreciation that "you can't do it alone" is growing. As a result, outreach efforts toward partnerships have received positive responses, particularly when goals and objectives are related to the needs of children, women, families, and the environment. Even corporations and foundations that are committed to being socially responsive are willing to explore potential for partnering. The challenge is to emphasize UNICEF/LA's commitment to the local community as well as to the global arena.

- The Children's Holiday Celebration was a concert put on in partnership with the city of Los Angeles Master Chorale, with script and music designed to celebrate cultural differences through the use of choral music. The concert featured special guests. Other participants included the Los Angeles Unified School District, the Independent Schools Association, L.A. County Probation Department, the "Tree People" environmental organization and the Los Angeles Housing Authority. The corporate partners were Hanna Barbera, Toys R Us, and Farley Candies. A local education grant was given by Parsons Foundation to UNICEF/LA and the Master Chorale to promote multicultural education in the Los Angeles community.

In the October 13, 1994, Los Angeles *Herald Dispatch*, Marilyn Solomon, the executive director of UNICEF/LA, summarizes her organization's approach: "I believe community partnerships can contribute to improving the condition of children. I see my role as matchmaker. As the world grows smaller, it is important for us to recognize that we can all work together on behalf of the world's children."

What Solomon and her enthusiastic and committed volunteer leadership team are doing is reaching out to those corporate leaders who believe in UNICEF/LA's mission, want to make a difference, and want to be counted among corporate citizenry doing good works. Solomon and her corps of volunteers are also not selfish. They, too, are committed to the missions of other LA-based nonprofits and believe reverently that sharing is more effective than competing in today's world.

Such partnering and collaboration, although picking up momentum in the nonprofit sector as a whole, are fraught, unfortunately, with difficulty. As David W. Battey, president of the fledgling and rapidly expanding Youth Volunteer Corps of America said in a recent interview, "I think sometimes people get so committed to their organization, and their mission, and their logo, and their name, that it's hard for them to look beyond that. Envy and jealousy are also natural human responses that can make collaboration difficult."

When contemplating a partnership with a nonprofit or a corporate entity, remember to

- Define clearly what the exchange of value will be between and among the partnering entities and what each brings to the table. Be specific.
- Determine whether the relationship requires a legal framework and articles of understanding or whether the relationship is an informal one. Examples of an informal partnership include joint fund-raising efforts, event sponsorships, and the like. Such relationships are typically for a time or date and specific in nature rather than on a day-to-day basis.
- Make sure that the missions of the collaborating organizations are compatible. For example, you would not look to corporate sponsorship from a tobacco firm if you were developing programs or engaged in fund-raising activities for a substance abuse program for juveniles.
- Make sure everyone in the partnering organizations (including the boards) understands the nature of the relationship.

CREATING STRATEGIC ALLIANCES

Growing numbers of nonprofit organizations are working jointly and in collaboration with other nonprofits as well as with for-profit corporations. This new trend is borne primarily of the belief that the replication of existing programs and services with a subtle twist here or there is not in the overall best care-and-service providing interests of the nonprofit sector, nor is it financially feasible.

The case study that follows provides some groundbreaking thinking on how to formulate a strategic alliance with entities of good will and complementary missions.

CASE STUDY

A Strategic Alliance Borne of the Arts and Industry

Maureen Weiss, "Kohler Company's Arts/Industry Residential Program for Artists," *Across the Board*, May 1992, p. 42.

Art and industry are not, contrary to their traditional reputations, incongruous work partners. Kohler Company, located in Kohler, Wisconsin, has known this since 1974, when, in celebration of its centennial, it started its Arts/Industry program as a four-week residency. Run in tandem with the John Michael Kohler Arts Center, the program now annually sponsors about fifteen artists-in-residence to work on average, four-month stints in the Kohler factories alongside Kohler workers. The artists, who come from all over the United States, are selected on the basis of the quality of their work, the feasibility of their proposals, the potential impact of the residency on their art, their technical skills, and their ability to work with Kohler employees.

The company, one of the nation's largest producers of plumbing fixtures, gives artists studio space, free materials, full run of the equipment, and technical assistance in its factories. The facilities, which are open twenty-four hours a day, include a pottery and enamel shop and brass and iron foundries. Because of the prohibitive costs of foundries and other equipment, the program provides many artists with their only chance to experiment on a large scale with many industrial materials, especially metals. Kohler also provides artists with housing and a weekly stipend to cover basic living costs.

In return, artists are required to spend one day of each month of their residency teaching art education to different community groups. They are also asked to give one work each to Kohler and the John Michael Kohler Arts Center. The artists are allowed to keep all the other work they produce during their residency.

Says Ruth Kohler, the director of the John Michael Kohler Arts Center, "Since the program began, workers and their families have become involved in the arts center: attending lectures, sending their children to art classes, going on trips to museums. Many of them have developed extensive art collections from the work of resident artists."

Although Ruth Kohler wished that there were a closer daily working relationship between the program artists and the company's engineers and designers, the Arts/Industry program has left its mark on the products made by the factory workers. The artists' experimentation with decorating toilets, bathtubs, and sinks with marbleized glazes, colored clays, and decals has led to Kohler's Artist Editions product line. The line, launched in 1985 as an off-shoot of the Arts/Industry program, used designs made by artists in the program. Today it is a full-product division consisting of four separate collections of bath products, one of which—the Personalities Line—still uses designs made by resident artists. Other designs are created by the corporate design staff.

Ironically, the artists have left their mark not only on bathtubs but on Kohler workers as well. This leaves Ruth Kohler convinced that the program could be reproduced in any manufacturing company, but she cautions that its success depends on strong administrative support:

> It's hard for artists and workers to speak each other's language, yet the key to the value and success of this program is the relationship between the artists and the factory workers. A company could not just give an artist some money and free use of its factory; there needs to be an intermediary—in this case the John Michael Kohler Arts Center—to provide administrative support and, more importantly, to act as a translator between the two sides to help them work together.

The second case study is of an entity in its nascent stages that is seeking foundation support to launch it into its second stage of development.

CASE STUDY

Charting New Territory

In 1993, Brian Gorman applied his years of professional experience and his passion for creating new and unorthodox approaches to solving societal ills to the overwhelming problem of AIDS. In a fundraising case statement entitled the AIDS Futures Initiative: A Strategy for Responding to AIDS in America (January 1993), Mr. Gorman writes:

The AIDS Futures Initiative (AFI) is proposed as an alternative approach for responding to AIDS in America. AFI is a not for profit organization established for the purpose of defining a unified national AIDS strategy. In fulfilling its purpose, the AIDS Futures Initiative looks at AIDS from a systemic perspective.

The AIDS Futures Initiative is a new and unique venture. The territory it is entering is largely uncharted. While the purpose is clear, the course is not. AFI is an organization which will never be large in size, but will touch the life of every American through its work.

What Gorman makes abundantly clear in the fundraising case statement he has generated to support his grant applications to philanthropic organizations is that AFI is not to compete with, or supplant, other AIDS organizations and the services they provide. Rather, it is to establish a *series* of strategic alliances. As he described in an interview with the author of this text in April 1995:

> The services of AFI are designed to be used as an integrated component of decision-making and action taken by our clients across all sectors. Our services are intended to support individuals and collaborative decision-making and action. The AIDS Futures Initiative is different in that we are seeking to support the development of resilient approaches to AIDS at the individual, organizational, and social levels across all sectors. Our business plan does not call for a replication of the efforts of others. Rather, we will work to form strategic alliances which allow us to apply the skills and wisdom of those organizations in the achievement of the AIDS Futures Initiatives mission.

We can glean from the early pioneers who have created a strategic alliance with another nonprofit, for-profit, or governmental agency a few salient points for your organization to keep in mind in creating such relationships:

- These relationships are founded on trust and goodwill. The boards and executive directors alike must recognize the unique qualities, attributes, programs, and services the other entity can bring to the table.

- Strategic alliances are necessarily mission based and outcome complementary; their focus is to provide constituents with optimal and seamless service.
- Strategic alliances are necessarily fluid in nature. The duration of the relationship is dependent primarily on the synergy it creates on behalf of the constituents, the vision of the two aligned organizations, and the volunteer and staff leadership of the entities.

Divesting Costly Overhead Structures and Services

Yet another way in which nonprofit organizations are reengineering relationships is through contracting out ancillary and support activities. For years, health care organizations, colleges and universities, schools, and other nonprofits have allowed contracts for the provision of food services, custodial services, elevator repair, payroll processing, major renovation, and architectural services. Typically, for-profit entities provided these services.

Growing numbers of nonprofits are now exploring ways to share costly overhead expenses with other nonprofit organizations by developing a consortium of similar institutions. For example, rather than maintaining their own printing services operations, Lindsay DesRochers, vice president for finance and administrative services at Portland State University, has contracted for those services from the nearby Oregon Health Sciences University. Not only does she report improved service levels, but also a substantial savings to the administrative overhead of the campus. The University of Massachusetts has a collaborative procurement center that enables the officers from the various campuses to directly place orders centrally to realize economic gains through on-line volume purchasing and improved service levels.

Yet others are asking why their nonprofit even engages in other than core mission activities; they believe that the nonprofit's sole responsibility should be doing what it was founded to do: generate quality programs and services germane to its mission. The functional areas of responsibility that fall under Don Bruegman's domain as senior vice president of Virginia Commonwealth University include facilities management, auxiliary enterprises, finance, accounting, procurement, technology and communications. In a January 1995 interview with the author of this text he asked dramatically:

> Why should my position exist? The only reason the University exists is to fulfill its teaching, research and public service mission. What I and the hundreds of staff reporting to me do is make the

University function on a day-to-day level so that students can earn a degree and the faculty can teach and conduct their research. I am convinced that there are individuals and firms out there who have the technical expertise to provide the University the operating service support it needs better and cheaper than I can, given the administrative barriers I face in a public entity. I say, do away with my job, contract out all of the services my staff provide and put in place a competent contract manager who can negotiate the contracts, assess the vendor's on-going capability of delivering a high quality service, and firing the vendor, if needed.

Certainly a radical response. But is it far fetched? Probably not. Indeed, there may be some wisdom in Bruegman's insights. Regardless of whether you are willing to go all the way, as Bruegman suggests, or whether you are willing to take only one operation at a time and consider it for outsourcing by a vendor, remember that

- Contracting out with another nonprofit or private vendor is only as good as the process you undertake to determine which services should be outsourced. Further, remember that this is a business decision that requires specifications stipulating the services and service levels expected of the vendor, the length of the contract, and the operating principles.
- The stories you hear from your colleagues about failed attempts to outsource such activities are due in large measure to a failed process of initially hiring the vendor and an ongoing failure to insist the vendor live up to the terms of the contract.
- Contracting out for services has a major impact on the lives of staff members and their families and, consequently, on the morale of the charity.

MORAL IMPERATIVES AND THE PROFIT MOTIVE: CONTRADICTORY OR COMPATIBLE?

Throughout this chapter, we have provided new ways for nonprofits to think about their structure and the delivery of their mission-based programs and services to multiple constituents. To that end, we have described mergers, strategic alliances, and partnerships. There are two additional means available to the nonprofit to reengineer the manner in which programs and services are delivered with an eye toward increased profit: the creation of for-profit spin-offs, and the transformation of a nonprofit into a for-profit entity. The latter is perhaps the most radical of all the reengineering alternatives.

For-profit spin-offs are not unknown to the new nonprofit sector. For example, a growing number of nonprofits create for-profit entities with separate boards of directors to run retail operations that serve as outlets for goods that carry the nonprofit's logo but are not specifically aligned with the mission of the 501 (C) (3) nonprofit organization. Such spin-offs have also been designed to run everything from operations that provide fee-for-service consulting services (examples include Girl Scouts of America and Catalyst, the nonprofit dedicated to conducting research on the status of women in the workplace) to member and nonmember organizations like the Harvard Coop and other bookstore/retail organizations to real estate holding companies (examples include Harvard, Columbia, and New York Universities).

Although such arrangements can generate profit for the support of the nonprofit entity itself, boards and executive directors alike need to learn some tough lessons from their colleagues:

- Spin-offs require due diligence at every level of your organization, from the board of directors to the executive director, to the directors, and to those delivering the product or service.
- The entity requires businesspeople with a business mentality for generating profit.
- The entity requires a detailed business plan with market-driven benchmarks, staff training and development programs, competitive wages, incentive plans, and career tracks.
- The executive director and the board of the nonprofit entity need to ensure the financial integrity of the nonprofit and the for-profit spin-off. They need desperately to avoid what happened to the for-profit spin-off from United Way of America, Partnership Umbrella Inc., in which the federal government accused the president and the two former chief financial officers of using the spin-off as a vehicle for diverting charitable funds.

As indicated previously, nonprofits have historically viewed the blending of nonprofit and profit motives as oxymoronic or suspicious at best. The financial conditions confronting many grassroots organizations are so daunting, however, that a number of social entrepreneurs are transforming their nonprofit agencies into business ventures with a social mission. Such ventures to date can be categorized as either affirmative or direct-service businesses.

In a thought-provoking article in the March 1995 issue of *Across the*

Board (pp. 20–25), Jerr Boschee, president and CEO of Alpha Center for Social Entrepreneurs Inc., a nonprofit organization founded to encourage entrepreneurship among nonprofits and expand social-purpose business ventures, defines *affirmative businesses* as those "created to provide real jobs, competitive wages, and career opportunities and ownership for people who are disadvantaged, whether it be physically, mentally, economically, or educationally." Boschee reports that approximately 60 percent of such employees are physically, visually, or hearing disabled; mentally retarded or mentally ill; members of inner-city minority groups; and recovering substance abusers.

Direct-service businesses, on the other hand, are created to serve a target population, such as emotionally troubled children, battered women, and people who are terminally ill.

Boschee aptly describes the challenges facing the social entrepreneur:

> Affirmative-business entrepreneurs must compete in the marketplace against companies that do not employ people who are disadvantaged; direct-service entrepreneurs must survive in a skewed market where the people receiving services [the clients] are usually not the people paying for them [the customers]. . . . On the surface, affirmative businesses appear to be starting at a competitive disadvantage. . . . But the pioneers in the field have been successful for two primary reasons: (1) They refuse to underestimate their workers; and (2) they are doggedly market-focused. . . .
>
> As for direct service entrepreneurs, the gulf between clients and customers has long daunted social-service providers. But social entrepreneurs have repeatedly demonstrated an ability to identify and attract appropriate sources of third party payment, ranging from government fee-for-service contracts (as opposed to government subsidies) to family members, insurance companies, corporations and others. (p. 22)

The next case study describes how a nonprofit organization emerged as a for-profit with impressive quantative and bottom-line results.

CASE STUDY

Social Entrepreneurs, Managers of Moral Imperatives
Affirmative Business: Cooperative Home Care Associates

Nine years ago, Rick Surpin and his colleagues at a South Bronx community-development agency were facing two overwhelming problems: They were trying to create permanent jobs for hard-to-employ black and Latino women in their community, and they were trying to do it in an industry with a reputation for low pay, high turnover, and inconsistent service.

Despite the obstacles, Cooperative Home Care Associates, a for-profit enterprise, has grown from a startup to a $5 million business employing about 300 women. The company provides home health care services for people who are elderly and disabled, and it offers employees full-time jobs with above-average pay and benefits, career mobility, and profit sharing. Wages, among the industry's highest, average $7 per hour for new workers and $8 for veteran workers, with annual bonuses ranging from $200 to $500. Six of the ten seats on the board of directors are held by elected employees.

The company won the National Business Enterprise Trust award in 1992 and is expanding to four other cities.

Direct-Service Business: Vitas Health Care Corp.

One of the more financially successful social-purpose business ventures started in 1976 when Hugo A. Westbrook, a minister, and Esther Colliflower, a nurse teaching at a Miami community college, developed an innovative curriculum in death education and started a hospice to care for the terminally ill. They set up their first office in the basement of a church and started without any capital except sweat equity.

Most of the patients are visited regularly in their homes by an interdisciplinary team comprised of a doctor, nurse, certified home health aide, social worker, chaplain, and volunteer. Helping patients cope with both physical and emotional pain is typically the goal. For more complex cases, a patient may be admitted to one of the company's homelike inpatient facilities, where visiting hours are unlimited, surroundings are friendly, and families—even pets—are allowed to stay.

Today, Vitas Health Care Corp. is a $150 million business offering palliative care for people who are terminally ill. The company has provided hospice services to more than 75,000 people and currently serves patients in nine states.

Although the company was initially structured as a nonprofit organization, Westbrook and Colliflower insisted it be run like a business, generating enough income from operating revenues to be financially sound. They also worked hard to enact key legislation licensing Florida hospices. In doing so, Westbrook was a leading figure in establishing the first—and still used—standards of quality for the care of people who are terminally ill. That effort led three years later to passage by Congress of Medicare reimbursement of hospice services nationally. Shortly thereafter, Westbrook converted the business to for-profit status, primarily to secure the venture capital needed for expansion.

There remain those who are not prepared for a radical redesign that abandons the tax-exempt world. For those of you who want to function as nonprofit entrepreneurs and are willing to rethink your core lines of business, we offer the following advice:

- Conduct a strategic assessment/portfolio analysis (see Chapter 2) from the perspective of both the mission and bottom line.
- Focus on the nonprofit's most effective mission-based programs and market demand and be willing to intentionally reallocate resources—that is, invest, divest, or maintain current service delivery levels.
- Become less dependent on governmental subsidies and individual and corporate philanthropy. Investigate new ways in which to generate revenues.

CHAPTER EIGHT

The Performance Measurement Conundrum

As nonprofits reengineer the manner in which they fulfill their missions and serve their constituents, they labor under public scrutiny. Such public scrutiny, jaded by the management and director debacles of the NAACP and the United Way, is on the increase. Indeed, these and other converging issues that plague the nonprofit sector (for example, the rising costs of health care, the failure to provide programmatic safety nets for young children in child care, the abuse of children by the clergy) have poisoned public opinion. No longer are nonprofits perceived as uniformly performing "good works." No longer are nonprofits unequivocally held in high esteem by those who are served by them.

These days, the public and the media are bringing accountability into the open. Demands for accountability come from various sectors: (1) the public, the beneficiaries of the world of the nonprofit; (2) donors, whose money is dedicated to a certain cause; (3) the government, whose interest is ensuring that charities do not abuse their tax-exempt status; and (4) the watchdogs, those agencies that influence, regulate, and control the sector.

Experience tells us that the nonprofit has not been successful in defining meaningful performance measures. This is due in large part to the diversity and complexity of the sector and, frankly, the absence of sustained pressure from the public, directors, and media to do so. We believe the picture has changed dramatically, however, because of the recent emphasis on accountability. The logic is simple: If a nonprofit evaluates its operations and develops strategies for correcting weaknesses, then it becomes more efficient, and in turn does better at keeping its promises to constituents, and thereby becomes more accountable.

The goal of this chapter is to ask questions about how to engage in performance management. The concepts of *benchmarking* and *best practices* are presented and contrasted in the first half of this chapter. The second half of the chapter provides the reader with a general framework or performance report card that can be tailored to the specific needs of the nonprofit.

BENCHMARKING: CRITICAL DATA FOR DECISION MAKING OR COMFORT ZONE FOR DIRECTORS AND STAFF?

Benchmarking compares the cost and effectiveness of one organization's operations to those of other organizations. Operations are typically defined as some activity, function, or process. This externally driven approach gives staff and volunteers the opportunity to determine how their particular nonprofit organization fares within certain broad-based measures.

Given the extraordinary cry for public accountability, nonprofit directors and senior staff have begun to collect such benchmarking data in order to answer critics' questions and to understand which activities fall within the band of cost effective operations and those that are off-scale. Collecting such data is no easy task. First, the nonprofit must identify those organizations that are most similar to its own with regard to mission and service objectives. The identification of such a peer group often includes factors of budget size, number of staff, contributed income, the amount of earned income (dollars raised through membership fees, user fees, retail operations, etc.), and other criteria deemed important for comparability.

In some cases, nonprofits also choose to identify those organizations that they admire or aspire to become. In yet other cases, they look to corporate models. These corporate models are used to examine the effectiveness and efficiency of such processes as invoicing, personnel action form processing, and procurement (purchasing and accounts payable). Such business processes, in the eyes of some staff and directors, are fundamentally the same in the for-profit and nonprofit and, therefore, worthy of comparison and analysis.

The health care and higher education sectors of the nonprofit have developed methodologies to capture such data. Indeed, health care providers have created and utilized such benchmarks for years. In higher education, the National Association of College and University Business Officers (NACUBO) undertook a first-of-a-kind benchmarking project in 1992. The objective of NACUBO's project was to develop benchmarks for each of the major administrative support functions (excluding teaching and learning in the classroom) found in a college or university setting. In turn, these major functions (admissions, for example) were assigned certain key processes and activities (e.g., application process from point of original inquiry to initial acknowledgment of receipt of application by the university, to notification of admission and financial aid packaging, to student intent to enroll, to matriculation). Next, data were gathered on an institution-by-institution basis to indicate the number of people (full-time equivalent) involved in a particular activity or process over a stated period of time and the volume of transactions (e.g., the number of days required to turn around an applicant's request for admission material, the number of financial aid packages completed by one full-time employee during a day).

Approximately 160 out of a total of 3,200 higher education institutions have participated in the NACUBO project. In many ways, this startling statistic speaks to the complexity of benchmarking not only in higher education but in the nonprofit world as a whole. Indeed, NACUBO is currently deciding whether to scuttle the project or totally redesign it. What went wrong? Nothing specifically. In fact, we commend NACUBO for its risk taking. What did go awry, however, were some fundamental assumptions about how higher education works and perceives itself. Fundamentally, most colleges and universities believe they are unique and, therefore, there's little to be learned from other such institutions.

However, there are some telling lessons to be learned from those chief administrative and financial officers who participated in the extensive data-gathering efforts. These lessons are totally applicable to the performing and cultural arts nonprofits, social services agencies, relief agencies, schools, and others.

- The nonprofit is not output driven. As discussed earlier in this text, what nonprofits do typically does not manifest itself uniformly or with immediate result. For example, it takes years of discipline and training to become a concert pianist. As a consequence, it requires longitudinal study to determine the success of the graduate, to compare one student's experience with others at the conservatory, and, finally, to identify what made the difference.

- Many nonprofits may have mission statements that, on the surface, sound strikingly similar, but they go about the actual delivery of that mission to their constituents in a myriad of ways. Take, for example, the world of nongovernmental organizations that are considered international relief agencies. Save the Children, CARE, Catholic Relief Services, Christian Children's Fund, and the U.S. Committee for UNICEF all serve children in developing countries, yet each organization addresses health and survival needs of these children differently in the field. Some are recipients of U.S. Agency for International Development (AID) money and run field operations themselves. Others rely on a parent organization to provide the hands-on provision of field services. Yet others rely on the monthly sponsorship of children by interested donors.

- Executive directors and their senior staff often do not believe that data on such operating characteristics as number of staff, types of clients served, mission, and size of budget truly is comparable. What emerges is often a caveat-driven explanation for every indicator (i.e. those entities with similar operating characteristics) or benchmark studied. For example, one of the common benchmarks employed is the cost of fund-raising. Many social service organizations aspire to spend ten cents for every dollar raised. However, what gets counted as overhead may vary. One agency may include both its central fund-raising staff and those staff resident in chapters/local associations. Another may include only the staff component of the central fund-raising and development function. Consequently, many believe the data are of marginal utility.

- The degree to which various functions, activities, and processes are automated varies significantly within one nonprofit, let alone among a peer group. In many cases, information technology has played a critical role in improving performance and productivity. Breakthroughs in software and database technology have enabled the nonprofit sector to generate, disseminate, analyze, and store information from more sources and for more users more quickly and less expensively. Most typically these services are found in the generation of monthly financial reports, payroll, invoice processing, and related finance functions. However, few nonprofits have the technology to support a pledge/accounts receivable system and/or a donor acknowledgment system. Even greater number of nonprofits have minimal technological support to monitor client/user progress (e.g., successful completion of a substance abuse program or the number of children provided rehydration tablets who otherwise would have died in underdeveloped countries). As a consequence, reporting benchmarking data without an explanation of the degree of automation and the degree to which the front end user is on-line will produce information of limited utility.

- It takes a lot of hard work and effort across organizational lines to determine what constitutes a particular function, activity, and process, and it is often difficult to reach a consensus about who should take a role in its execution and how long it should take to complete the particular function, activity, or process. These are the questions that are raised in an activity-based cost model to determine the cost of providing a service or program. There are, in fact, many commercially available software packages to undertake such analysis. Once again, however, caution must be exercised. First, be aware that activity-based cost models are subjective: They ask employees or volunteers to indicate how they perceive their time is spent. Second, some of the packages include an employee's total compensation (base salary plus benefits), while others include only the base salary. Again, it's an issue of comparing apples with apples and oranges with oranges, internally first and then from organization to organization.

- Even those sectors that have been engaged in the development and application of benchmarking typically find the number of peer participants is not sufficient to provide enough data for relevant comparison. As indicated earlier, less than 200 institutions participated in at least one complete round of NACUBO's benchmarking. A representative of a small, co-ed liberal arts institution may not find enough participating institutions to warrant the thousands of person hours required to participate in the benchmarking survey in the first place.

This litany of lessons is meant neither to imply that benchmarking is impossible to undertake nor to suggest that the data generated through such a project are useless. Indeed, benchmarking has its virtues. It provides managers, directors, and the nonprofit's various publics the opportunity to identify targets for change or celebrate processes efficiently conducted. In contrast with internal yardsticks that focus on the measurement of current performance in relation to prior period results, current budget, or the results of other departments within the nonprofit, benchmarking can have an eye-opening effect for staff and volunteers alike. Simply put, it forces them to consider how other organizations run their daily operations and carry out their mission.

There is, however, a fundamental flaw in nonprofit sector benchmarking. To date, there are all too few organizations that have exercised the will to reengineer their fundamental functions, activities, and processes. As a consequence, nonprofit benchmarking measures one group's performance against that of another that is probably not exemplary itself. In essence, measuring one cumbersome and convoluted process against another to determine which is the best of the worst, the middle of the worst, or the worst of the worst is a feeble attempt to improve management. That is why we strongly believe that, currently, there is little return on investment for engaging massive amounts of time and resources in collecting internal data and participating in external comparative analyses. Although such benchmarking data may provide a comfort or discomfort zone for staff and directors, there is a far more cogent approach to developing meaningful performance measures—the establishment of best practices.

REENGINEERING PERFORMANCE MEASUREMENT

What is a best practice? A *best practice* is defined as the most cost effective method for carrying out a process or providing a service. This is in contrast with benchmarking, which compares the cost and effectiveness of one group's operations to those of one or more other organizations. The key, operative phrase in the definition of best practice is *most cost effective.*

Determining what is most cost effective is, in fact, an exemplary way of providing service or engaging in a process, but it is no simple task. One reason that financial measures are more reliable and, therefore, carry more weight is that they are assumed to be uniformly defined (generally accepted accounting principles concerning fund accounting have provided this fundamental standard of measurement). This allows for a comparison of financial results across a nonprofit's units, divisions, and affiliates, and with other selected organizations. As we have discussed, however, these measures are not uniformly or consistently comparable despite the thousands of hours invested in efforts to make them so because nonprofits and their accountants sometimes interpret accounting conventions in subtle yet different ways. Given this reality and the others enumerated earlier in this chapter, it is easy to see why developing additional and nonfinancial measures that executive directors and their boards can use will be an undertaking of gargantuan proportions.

It is clear that as long as one well-respected nonprofit organization within each of the sectors can demonstrate the long-term advantage of its superior performance (quality programs and services), innovative delivery mechanisms, or cost effective ways of providing core mission programs, it will change the performance standards of comparable organizations. And with so many new players and providers of service on the scene, the pressure for distinguishing programs and services through thoughtful performance measurement is growing exponentially. Once again, it is a bottom-line issue. Nonprofits must compete for limited financial resources and prove to potential donors that they will realize a greater return on their investment if they give to one particular nonprofit as opposed to others that espouse a similar mission and vision.

Developing a best practices approach requires some thought-provoking discussion among the senior staff and directors about who should lead/direct the development of such a performance measurement system. One option is to assign responsibility to the executive director or a member of the senior management team (the chief operating officer, for example). The other option is to assign this effort to a steering committee or oversight body that has been assigned responsibility for reengineering efforts. This steering committee and its associated teams have become intimately familiar with the inner workings of your nonprofit and have redesigned the administrative processes as well as service and program delivery; therefore, they are probably best equipped to redefine performance management with new principles. Some past practices may still be the most appropriate for your group, but everything should be strenuously challenged. Otherwise, your efforts will yield incremental results at best. For example, you may streamline your organization's purchasing process but have chosen to hold off on streamlining the accounts payable portion of the process to a later time.

Throughout this book, we have talked about the need to create and embrace clearly focused and articulate mission and vision statements. They provide the road map or template for reengineering all aspects of your nonprofit. We have also described the fundamental elements for human resource management for successfully implementing reengineering. Therefore, the newly crafted performance measures must be linked to a new accountability and reward system based much more heavily on group, rather than individual, performance (see Chapter 2 for a discussion of reengineering the budget/resource allocation process and Chapter 6 for reengineering compensation and classification systems). Such a performance system, in turn, requires the technology to support it at both the most senior administrative levels and at the front-line where staff interact directly with constituents.

Current performance measurement systems employed throughout the sector pose significant barriers to change. In the nonprofit sector, watchdog agencies and accrediting and certifying agencies typically focus on

- *Short-Term Financial Measures.* Typically, board members and senior staff react reflexively to the bottom line of the annual operating budget rather than focusing on long-term financial viability or equilibrium. As a consequence of being fixated on breaking even within the operating budget, the fundamental economic needs (operating expenses plus investments in physical plant, equipment, technology, training, and development) of the organization are not considered for the future. Consequently, the organization is not able to get itself out from under operating shortfalls or breakeven budgets.

- *Internal Management Accounting Systems.* These management accounting systems are based on the external reporting requirements enumerated by the Financial Accounting Standards Board (FASB) and by watchdog agencies. Unfortunately, the financial measures that such agencies have developed provide only a measure of short-term financial stability. Finally, consulting firms and watchdog agencies are becoming more attuned to the need to assess both the current financial health and the service components of nonprofit organizations. They now realize that it is essential to understand not only the financial viability of the nonprofit but the value (as expressed through its services and programs) it provides its constituents.

There are several additional factors that have not been the subject of external assessment but should be because they underscore some of the unique attributes of the sector.

Specifically, nonprofits typically do not assess a value to the time provided by volunteers and, subsequently, the value in both financial and psychological terms to the constituent. Although time is a most precious commodity in these days of information overload and expectations of immediate response, it is that very time and commitment to securing constituents and providing programs that contribute or create the most fundamental value of the organization.

In the long run, the people who are committed to a nonprofit's mission and who are serving selflessly are the most valuable asset of the organization. In many groups, it is ironic that those who are on the front line serving constituents are among these poorest paid and least valued. High turnover among these workers is not only expensive in terms of recruiting and training new staff and volunteers, it often undermines the nonprofit's ability to maintain a consistently high level of service.

The design of new models for measuring performance among the nonprofit sectors must look beyond short-term, financial measures to include the following factors:

Mission Based. Social and human values, rather than financial results, complicate performance measurement. The centrality of mission for nonprofits necessarily places limits on their ability to be flexible. Dollars can be secured in a variety of ways, but social and human values cannot. In the future, performance measures must assess whether the organization is operating in the most effective manner possible as opposed to being a statement of good intentions.

Exchange of Value. Measurement of performance should be viewed through the eyes of the constituency the nonprofit serves. Recognizing the exchange of value between the nonprofit and the constituent will ensure that the donor, the volunteer, or the client remains loyal to the organization.

Quality. Performance measurement must routinely monitor quality from both internal and external perspectives. Quality is not necessarily easily quantified. Most often, quality is a composite of subjective measures and feelings of those either providing or receiving the service. Ultimately the nonprofit will have to ask the question: What specific service levels of quality do we want to continuously attain?

Outcomes. Outcomes are the ultimate test of any nonprofit. Every nonprofit exists to change and enhance people and society, but such results are difficult to measure. For example, the Salvation Army has strong and important religious tenets. The Salvation Army maintains statistics and other quantitative measures that indicate the number of alcoholics it has restored to mental and physical health as well as the number of criminals it has rehabilitated. The outcome of this overarching facet of their mission is terribly challenging to measure. However, there are specific programs where it is possible to measure successfully outcomes.

Integration of Cross-Functional Components. Flexibility and responsiveness can only be achieved if nonprofits move from being hierarchically driven organizations to being horizontal, cross-functional ones with appropriate supporting processes and technology. Measurement approaches, particularly those geared toward assessing volunteer and staff performance, must permit the integration of measures for quality, cost, and effort across the traditional boundaries and turf that characterize the nonprofit.

Continuous Improvement. The nonprofit of the future must be capable of continuously improving its performance to meet the standards of external agencies as well as its best practices measures. Measurement approaches must focus on the rate of change in performance as well as the level and quality of performance.

CREATING A PERFORMANCE REPORT CARD FOR THE NONPROFIT OF THE FUTURE

The nonprofit of the future needs to create a balanced report card that focuses on five categories of performance:

1. *Mission.* Broad-based and strategic measures appropriate to both internal management needs as well as external constituents (donors, volunteers, and clients) and accrediting, certifying agencies.
2. *Finances.* Broad-based financial measures that capture both current and long-term operating perspectives appropriate for internal

   management needs as well as external constituents and accrediting, certifying agencies.

3. *User/Constituent Satisfaction.* Overall performance of the nonprofit in delivering high levels of quality service.

4. *Administration.* The performance of those administrative processes that impact internal users (i.e., staff, recipients of services/programs, volunteers) as well as external constituents.

5. *Nonprofit Learning.* The capacity and ability of the nonprofit to improve and innovate on a continuous basis, both in the larger nonprofit marketplace as well as internally.

Exhibit 8–1 presents the five critical measures that comprise the nonprofit performance report card.

Let us now address more specifically the way to define these performance measures for the nonprofit of the future.

Constituent Satisfaction

The creation of value begins with the user and/or the constituent. Therefore, you should start reengineering your nonprofit's performance measures through the eyes of the user/constituent. Using your nonprofit's mission and vision statement as the point of departure, you should assess the following:

1. *Program and service delivery mechanisms and cycles.* Identify the basic elements of time and effort that define your ability to meet user/constituent needs and requirements.

   • New program/service development cycle. In the midst of developing new programs and services, ask the following questions:

     What does it take to create a new program?

     How many hours of staff and volunteer time will be required to develop the program?

     When will we know that this new program is meeting user needs?

   • "Cradle to grave"/continuum of services. When assessing how to best meet the needs of your constituents from the point of original contact to the sustenance of an ongoing relationship, ask:

     What kind of ongoing relationship do we want to create for our clients?

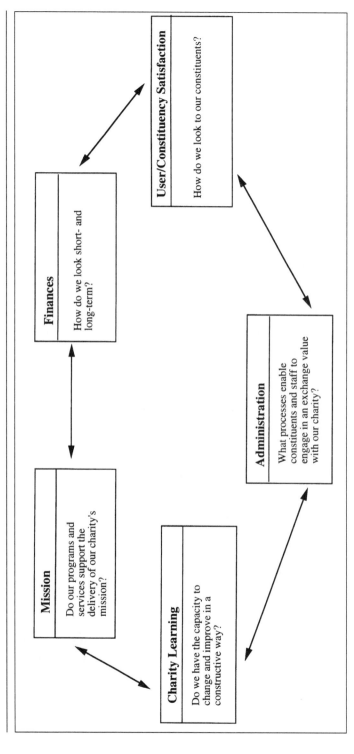

Mission

Do our programs and services support the delivery of our charity's mission?

Finances

How do we look short- and long-term?

User/Constituency Satisfaction

How do we look to our constituents?

Charity Learning

Do we have the capacity to change and improve in a constructive way?

Administration

What processes enable constituents and staff to engage in an exchange value with our charity?

Exhibit 8–1   The Nonprofit Performance Report Card

What constitutes the beginning of such a relationship and what should constitute the end of that relationship?

In the creation of a cradle-to-grave continuum of services, what is a supportive relationship with the nonprofit and what is a dependent, unhealthy one?

- Programs/service cycle. While identifying the time and effort required to support and maintain current service offerings, ask yourself:

Do we have the staff with the right skill sets and attitudes to work with our clients?

Are there tangible outcomes that result from particular services offered to our clients?

Are these outcomes positive for the client? Are the staff and volunteer efforts that have been required to provide this service worth the cost to our nonprofit?

2. *Quality.* Quality as perceived by the user/program and service recipient as well as those providing the program/service.

- Program/service quality.

What is the level of quality of the programs offered? The very best? Weak? Marginal?

How can we best secure the input of both service recipients and service providers to determine the quality of those programs offered?

What kind of investments need we make to ensure enhanced quality?

If our nonprofit's resources are limited, are we willing to drop those programs that are rated as poor or mediocre by service providers and clients alike?

- Service levels.

Are our clients provided the services they need at a time that is convenient for them rather than convenient for our staff?

Is the physical location and layout of our program convenient and user friendly to clients and staff alike?

Are we providing services consistently, at the right level (intensive, cursory), with the best volunteers and staff available, and with the proper frequency?

3. *Service.* Constituent/user satisfaction

- Gathering data regarding client satisfaction on a timely and consistent basis.

How do we create written and telephone opinion surveys that capture the essence of what our nonprofit does and how well it does it?

Are written surveys or telephone surveys more effective with our client base?

How do we go about determining what the best approach is?

Are user focus groups a good way of soliciting information from our clients?

If so, how do we go about identifying the right people to participate?

Do we need the expertise of opinion research gurus or can we develop the survey instruments ourselves with the help of volunteers and staff?

As the result of this kind of evaluation, your nonprofit will be able not only to assess the perceptions of those who both deliver and are the recipients of service but also to begin to establish best practices. As you become increasingly sophisticated in measuring user and provider satisfaction, you will be better equipped to compare your nonprofit's performance levels to those of similar organizations.

A word of caution about being constituent or user driven: Throughout this book, we have encouraged nonprofits to be mission based and constituency driven. Truly, we must value the input of our constituents. However, nonprofit managers and directors must also think carefully about what happens internally as they attempt to be responsive to constituents. Serving the constituent remains the proper objective, but it can happen only when managers and directors exercise the internal mission-based discipline to balance user desires and needs with nonprofit capacity.

Administration

In a nonprofit organization, traditional performance measures focus on narrow departments or functions, necessarily leading to fragmentation. To achieve new models for performance measurement, the nonprofit must view the organization as a system (see Chapter 2) made up of a number of intertwined program and service delivery mechanisms supported by an administrative infrastructure (comprised of processes, policies, procedures, and technology). Among those processes that support program and service delivery and require ongoing evaluation are

1. *Program and service design.* Very often, the creation and design of new programs are funded through external foundations and fund-

ing sources and require people on staff as well as volunteers who are versed in fund-raising grant-getting.

2. *Program and service development and delivery.* All nonprofits must take the initiative to ensure that newly crafted programs, as well as those that have been a part of its program portfolio, are meeting user needs.

3. *Marketing and nonprofit positioning.* As the nonprofit sector becomes increasingly competitive, it is critical that each group has in place those processes and support systems that promote aggressive marketing of its unique programs and services.

Using the mission and vision statements of the nonprofit, the administrative processes that have the greatest impact on constituent, volunteer, and staff satisfaction should next be identified. For each such administrative process, three measurement categories should be included:

1. *Cycle Time.* Determine the beginning to end time required to perform the process.

2. *Quality.* Define the critical milestones along the way for users as well as for staff and volunteers providing the service or delivering the program. Examples of quality include the graduation rate of undergraduates at a liberal arts university, the number of Nobel laureates on the faculty who have direct contact with undergraduates, growing number of congregates who are committed to and financially support the parish's Sunday school program, the number of patients who have been successfully treated for breast cancer and who show no recurrence of the disease five years after surgery and treatment.

3. *Productivity.* This oft dreaded concept in the nonprofit world must be addressed head on in this new approach to performance measurement. Clearly, nonprofits must be able to increase program and service outcomes. This means creating new measures for labor productivity or redefining productivity itself.

Once again, as is the case in the design of constituent satisfaction measures, standards of performance should be established through the use of best practices with peer and aspirant organizations and administrative processes.

Finances

Short-term financial measures that concentrate solely on this year's operating budget distort a nonprofit's long-term financial equilibrium.

Indeed, many a group has become dysfunctional with such a mind set. When reengineering financial performance measures for your nonprofit, adopt elements of the following framework to guide your deliberations:

Invest in longer term strategies, programs, and service, not in projects that are expected to generate immediate results.

Look at the impact of your decisions on cash flow.

Integrate a competitive strategy with a realistic picture of your group's finances.

Determine how much financial risk your nonprofit can assume. Growth, whether by internal expansion or through a merger, is sometimes too costly to achieve. Alliances and partnerships are less risky strategies, given the volatile nature of U.S. and world economies.

Nonprofit Learning

The willingness and capacity to continuously improve is strategic. In the nonprofit world, measuring the rate of change in performance (outcomes) is more important than measuring the absolute level of performance itself.

The ability to assess a product, or more appropriately, an outcome(s), in the nonprofit world is perhaps the most daunting task that will face you as you begin to reengineer your group's performance measures. This is largely due to the time required to generate an outcome in this sector. As American society as a whole and the nonprofit in particular become increasingly dependent on the knowledge-worker (see Chapter 6), nonprofits need to measure their volunteer and staff assets as well as more tangible, quantifiable ones. For example, rather than consider student credit hours generated by a faculty member or the number of cases carried by a social worker, it might be more appropriate to define what particular contribution/value an assistant professor or a part-time social worker imparts to learners or clients.

EMBEDDING PERFORMANCE MEASUREMENT IN AN INTENTIONAL MANAGEMENT PROCESS

It is simply not enough to develop new performance measures. Rather, the intrinsic value of performance measurement is derived from the broader management process in which it must be embedded. Such a management process must necessarily be driven by the mission and vision of the nonprofit and by an employee/volunteer resource management program that rewards and promotes cross-functional work tasks and continuous improvement.

As is the case with strategic planning, performance measures must be managed by the executive director and board leadership and must be linked directly to the nonprofit's mission and vision. Like strategic planning as well, establishing a performance measurement system requires an iterative process. Those associates (Chapter 6) who have front-line responsibility for transaction processing and working with constituents must provide input. All levels of employees and volunteers need to be involved in the design of the measurement criteria. In addition, senior leadership should circulate initial drafts to cross-functional work groups for their input, then modify the measurement system to reflect this input. Finally, such a performance management system should link directly with the employee compensation and performance measurement systems of your nonprofit. (See Chapter 6 for detailed discussion regarding employee and volunteer human resources systems.)

Although it may sound simplistic, any nonprofit contemplating the redesign of its performance management system (assuming that it has one in the first place) must have access to the information required to evaluate and improve its performance. As performance measurement touches every volunteer, every staff member, every user and constituent, a management information system and supporting technology are required to provide the requisite support at all levels throughout the organization.

First, the management information system of the future must provide the same sophistication for the assessment of quality, service, and cycle time as do many financial systems. Second, sophisticated databases will be required to reflect the integrated, team orientation of the new organization. In our view, how these measurement databases are managed will determine the success in implementing a performance measurement system.

The key questions to be asked in creating and implementing a new performance management system include the following:

- How does the nonprofit sector as a whole as well as the individual organization build the same kind of integrity into the measurement of nonfinancial performance as it has historically with financial performance measures?
- Who should be responsible for the creation, implementation, and continuous improvement of an integrated, cross-functional performance measurement system?
- How do nonprofits balance their own internal performance measurement needs with external forces—the public, foundations, and government agencies that demand quantifiable reports and donors who expect their dollars to be applied to the program most important to them?

- How do the executive director and the board communicate cogently about the factors that will create value in the future? How should external reports be crafted and provided to the external audience? What can be done to reformat annual reports to be more meaningful?

The nonprofit of the future has just begun to take shape. Senior staff and board leadership provide the greatest impact on such a group's mission and vision. What we measure conveys to the nonprofit and the world at large what is important. In short, if we measure it, it will happen.

CHAPTER NINE

Strategic Transformation: The Culmination of Reengineering

Throughout this text, we have described reengineering as a formal method for identifying and achieving fundamental performance improvements. We have left no stone unturned. We have talked about the inherent differences in reengineering the corporate and the nonprofit organization. We have described the role of strategic planning and strategic resource allocation as providing the template or framework for reengineering. The challenges and value that volunteers impart to the nonprofit have been enumerated, as has the need to reengineer the role and responsibility of the board and its relationship to the executive director.

The redesign of human resources management practices to unleash the passion and productivity of volunteers and staff, also has been espoused as the primary way in which to ignite fundamental change. Additionally, we have provided a conceptual framework for the reengineering of nonprofit management performance systems. To bolster further our arguments for the need to constantly redesign the nonprofit enterprise, we have presented dramatically different, bold, and exciting alliances and partnerships that nonprofits are beginning to pursue aggressively.

Although requiring an extraordinary degree of will and intestinal fortitude, reengineering results in a transformed organization. This final chapter promotes the need to look beyond today's focus on the fundamental yet invasive work steps associated with reengineering to those even bolder work steps associated with breaking down barriers to achieve nonprofit-wide transformation. *Carpe diem*! Seize the day, as the Romans said!

A FUNDAMENTAL SHIFT IN VOLUNTEER AND STAFF ACTIVITY

Administrative process reengineering and the reengineering of service delivery mechanisms focus on the very heart and soul of the nonprofit's mission. Organizational change as manifested in the flattening of reporting relationships, in the recognition that volunteers and staff at all levels must be held responsible and accountable for their actions, and in the understanding that the organization must work in an integrated fashion across traditional boundaries follows in response to the redesign of administrative processes and service delivery in support of the nonprofit's mission and vision. Without bold and committed staff an volunteer leadership, even these most fundamental of reengineering outcomes cannot be realized.

Transformation necessarily begins with reengineering the core mission and support activities. It reaches far beyond the immediate objective of improving performance. Transformation builds on the enhanced capabilities developed through reengineering to introduce yet more enhanced levels of service- and values-focused programs that can grow into new ventures, partnerships, or strategic alliances.

CHALLENGES TO CHANGE

As you can imagine, the transformation process, like any change process, is replete with challenges and barriers. Anticipation of these forces will go a long way to help reduce or eliminate resistance. Opportunity, as well as crisis and pain, emboldens leadership to change. The research conducted by Darryl Connor, president and CEO of the Atlanta-based firm, ODR, Inc., indicates that there are four fundamental challenges to change implementation efforts: culture, sponsorship, resistance, and change agents (Exhibit 9–1).

In any implementation effort, nonprofit staff and board members must be knowledgeable about their organization's culture and the degree to which there is the sponsorship or legitimacy for change. Research among corporate and nonprofit entities alike demonstrates that at least 60% of a nonprofit's implementation success rate depends on a thorough understanding of the organization's culture and the sponsorship provided for such change. The sponsorship for change needs necessarily to come from the highest levels of the organization, the executive director and the board. This gives change the legitimacy it needs to be successful.

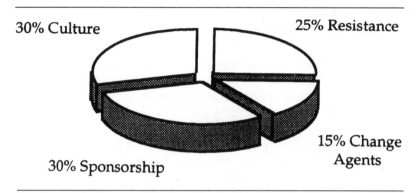

30% Culture

25% Resistance

15% Change Agents

30% Sponsorship

Exhibit 9–1 Challenges to Successful Implementation Efforts

In their role as sponsors, the executive director and the board members must deal with the natural resistance that will emerge from those volunteers and staff who are the actual targets of change. Typically, the senior management team and the board will appoint a small cadre of volunteers and staff who will be responsible for implementing change. These leaders are critical to the overall success of the implementation process because they work hand-in-hand with those who bear the brunt or are the targets of the change.

Reengineering and transformation represent fundamental change and, as such, are processes in which the nonprofit enters a transition state before it arrives at its desired goal. Exhibit 9–2 depicts the metamorphosis required.

In the present state, as shown in Exhibit 9–2 as a square, the organization's stability is depicted by a rigidly drawn box. This box, which has reached a point of organizational maturity, contains an operating environment that is familiar to its constituents.

This familiarity breeds considerable comfort among its constituents, even though the culture may not be universally respected or revered. In deciding to redesign its administrative processes, the nonprofit moves through a transition state in which old processes are streamlined and abandoned. During that transition state, newly reengineered processes are in a fluid state, being further refined and defined by the nonprofit's constituents. This state often evokes pain and is commonly described by organizational development specialists as unfreezing (pain) and refreezing (remedy). The transition state is characterized by low stability within the organization and among its constituents. It is normally replete

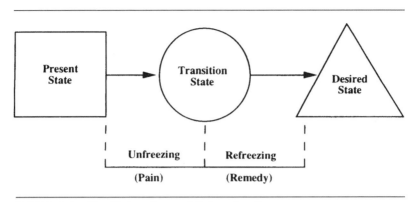

Exhibit 9–2 The Unfreezing and Refreezing Process

with emotional stress for volunteers, staff, and users/clients alike, and it is not at all unusual to see conflict develop and grow, sometimes at an exponential rate. As a result there is high, sometimes undirected volunteer and staff energy in which volunteers and staff alike look for fond, positive, and symbolic remembrances of the "good old days." This is also a time when who has control among and between volunteers and staff in the organization becomes a major bone of contention.

As newly reengineered processes take on a comfort level among the organization's staff and volunteers, the desired state is achieved and takes on a radically different form. This results, if you will, in "the" new way of doing work.

Strategies for Change

As you and your colleagues embrace the fundamental challenge you have prescribed in your reengineering efforts, be aware that there are four critical yet distinct roles that must be defined and intentionally exercised in order to achieve your goals of a new state:

1. Change Sponsor   The individual/group who legitimizes the change.
2. Change Agent   The individual/group who is responsible for implementing the change.
3. Change Target   The individual/group who must actually change.
4. Change Advocate The individual/group who wants to implement change but lacks sponsorship.

Also note, however, that the desired state is *not* a static state. Rather, the desired state is one that is and espouses continuous change.

Exhibit 9–3 enumerates those strategies and tactics designed to help you and your nonprofit manage your organization's reengineering and transformation efforts.

Responses to Change

Although you may believe that all the outward signs indicate you are successful in your change implementation efforts, both positive and negative changes will result in negative reactions from volunteers and staff, as well as those being served by your organization. Exhibit 9–4 portrays the curve that typically characterizes the fluctuations in mood and commitment experienced by volunteers and staff alike in any change over time. The time to be most wary is Phase 2, when your colleagues express doubt directly or indirectly and decide to check out, either by passively doing what they have always done or by leaving the organization for another that more clearly fits with their psychological, financial, and other creature comfort needs. Do not be frightened by this reaction. It is a normal one that will pass quickly if you are sensitive to the people, volunteers, and staff with whom you work. You should deal with such responses openly and publicly acknowledge your understanding of the feelings involved and articulate your own feelings about the proposed changes as well.

As occurs with any loss, changes that are perceived to be negative are replete with emotion. The ultimate key to your nonprofit's success in fundamental redesign is understanding the emotion of change and managing it in an active, open, supportive, and caring manner. Exhibit 9–5 powerfully depicts the emotional roller coaster you will ride as you implement the changes. The vertical axis depicts the degree of emotion which is apt to occur from the most passive to the most active state over time. Stability appears on the middle of the vertical axis to underscore the relatively neutral or comfortable state that is for most people. Overtime, as change is implemented, staff and volunteers will go from feeling fairly comfortable and safe within their operating environment, to feeling threatened and dysfunctional or immobilized. They will most likely feel anger about having to change and will begin to negotiate or bargain to satisfy their own anxiety about the change. Once the realization hits that change is to stay and will become the *modus operandi*, depression will set in until such time that the staff and volunteers maneuver through the implementation of change and once again becomes comfortable and accepts the new reality.

Unfreezing	Transition	Refreezing
Strategies		
Disavow the present state and promote movement away from existing expectation patterns.	Provide structure, guidance, confidence, and trust while encouraging movement.	Confirm the desired state and promote acceptance of new expectation patterns.
Tactics		
Explain the problems facing the nonprofit that have or will cause the status quo to no longer be viable	Reinforce the need for change and focus targets' attention on the future not the past.	Continue to demonstrate strong sponsorship of the change.
Outline the costs that will be incurred with the continued reliance on the status quo.	Encourage targets' self-confidence. Help them believe that they are capable of achieving the change and that the transition costs are more than compensated for by the benefits of the desired state.	Acknowledge the price targets paid during the transition, and highlight the emerging benefits of the new desired state.
Articulate and demonstrate strong sponsor commitment to the change.	Identify opportunities for sponsors to make symbolic decisions that send clear signals reinforcing the change.	Use consequence management: Rewards, Punishments, Effort
Reduce the targets' defensiveness about the past.	Provide as much accurate, timely information as possible.	
Specify the necessary changes.	Allow targets to vent their fears, concerns, insecurities, or grief in an environment that treats these feelings as legitimate.	
Use consequence management: Rewards, Punishment, Effort	Reward those who are supportive of the change and apply pressure to those who are resistant.	
	Assign roles, tasks, and responsibilities, so targets believe they are involved and exercising influence.	
	Provide targets with the logistic, economic, and political resources needed to achieve what you ask of them.	
	Identify anchors that targets can trust to remain constant and provide stability.	
	Provide targets with training in how to understand their own reactions, as well as the reactions of others.	

Exhibit 9-3 Strategies and Tactics Designed to Manage the Change

Response to Positive Change

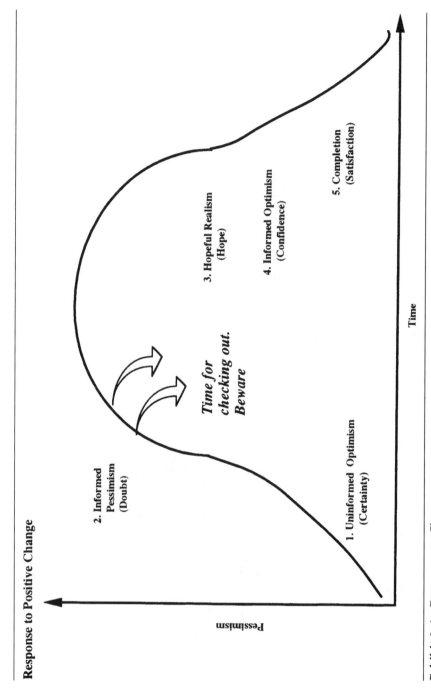

Pessimism

2. Informed
Pessimism
(Doubt)

*Time for
checking out.
Beware*

3. Hopeful Realism
(Hope)

4. Informed Optimism
(Confidence)

5. Completion
(Satisfaction)

1. Uninformed Optimism
(Certainty)

Time

Exhibit 9–4   Responses to Change

186

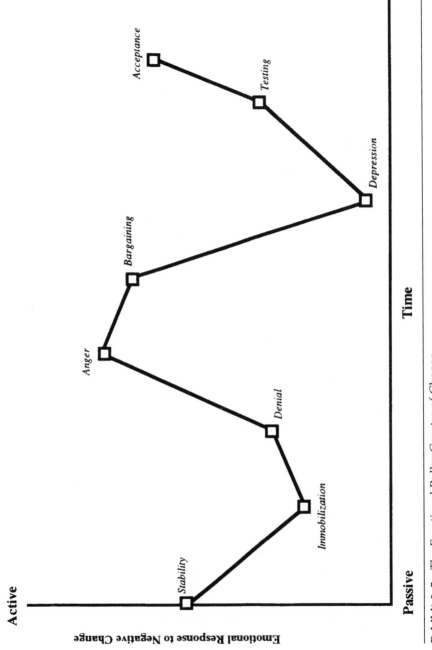

Exhibit 9–5 The Emotional Roller Coaster of Change

The bottom line for successful reengineering and transformation is commitment—commitment from the volunteers and staff of the non-profit itself. Exhibit 9–6 portrays the degree of support required to implement and internalize change over time.

There are three stages of commitment that volunteers and staff must experience in sequential order. These include preparation, acceptance, and commitment. These stages, which are depicted on the vertical axis of Exhibit 9–6, are contrasted with the learning and adaptation of volunteers and staff to change over time. For example, in the earliest stage of change, volunteers and staff are made privy to the proposed change. Some will be initially confused by the change; and as volunteers and staff come to understand the change, some will respond negatively. With the ongoing sponsorship of change at the executive director and board levels, those affected by the change will learn to adapt over time. Ultimately, the change will be institutionalized and individual staff and volunteers will buy into the change and internalize it.

The case that follows encapsulates the complexity and power of the human dynamic in a time of profound change.

CASE STUDY

The Cure for Cancer

To bring to light the emotion generated as the result of change, we present the impact the change process has had, continues to have, and will have on the American Cancer Society. Much of this case study focuses on the transformation of the relationship between the national and the local affiliates and the issue of funding the organization's fund-raising efforts.

The following is excerpted from "A Cure for the Cancer Society?," by Grant Williams (*Chronicle of Philanthropy*, July 17, 1994, pp. 32–34).

> Trying to stave off fund-raising problems and end bitter internal struggles, the American Cancer Society is putting the finishing touches on its most sweeping management shuffle in a half-century.
>
> Everyone involved with the society agrees that it has big problems. In three of the past four years, donations have not increased enough to keep pace with inflation. . . .What's more, the society faces intense competition from new groups that fight cancer and from other types of charities.

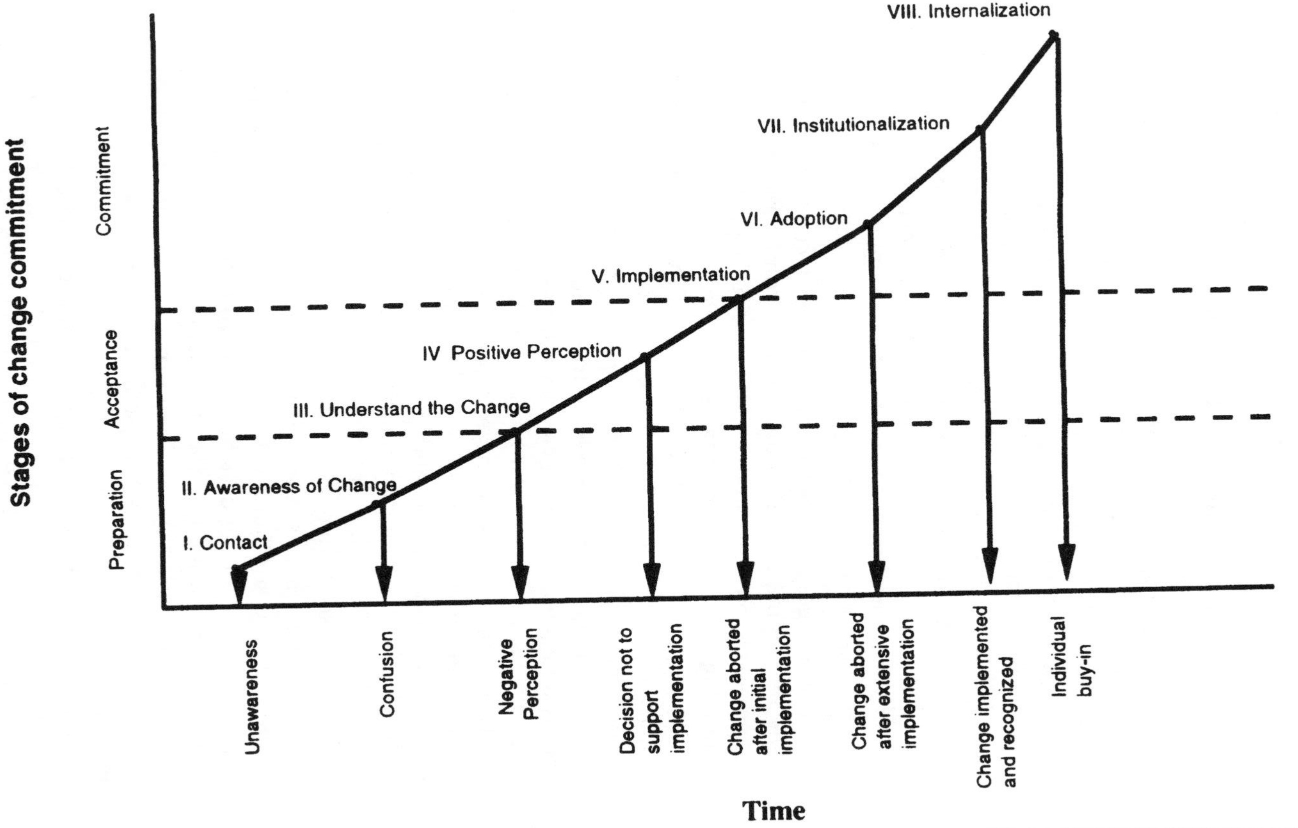

Stages of change commitment

Commitment
Acceptance
Preparation

VIII. Internalization
VII. Institutionalization
VI. Adoption
V. Implementation
IV Positive Perception
III. Understand the Change
II. Awareness of Change
I. Contact

Unawareness
Confusion
Negative Perception
Decision not to support implementation
Change aborted after initial implementation
Change aborted after extensive implementation
Change implemented and recognized
Individual buy-in

Time

Exhibit 9–6   Attaining Success Through Commitment

Many of the state and regional divisions have angrily protested the way the society is run. Some in the organization say frequent turnover in the society's top leadership over the past decade has caused the charity to drift.

To combat these problems—and to avoid a fall from grace—the Cancer Society has made major changes in the operations. It has:

- Revamped all of its departments—especially those that provide services to the fifty-seven state and regional divisions—and created six new offices.

- Started to return to the divisions some of the money they raised and passed on to the national office. The divisions are supposed to use the extra money to redouble their fund-raising.

Those changes stemmed from numerous recommendations made by committees of employees and volunteers, some of whom spent months studying the society's problems and examining how other big charities operate.

The overhaul has been widely praised by Cancer Society employees, leaders of its divisions and key volunteers. But many acknowledge that they have one lingering question: Will the changes work? John R. Seffrin, who has served as the society's national executive vice president—its top staff job— since 1992 says: "There is a big leap of faith . . . but we can say with some peace of mind and pride that we've done the right thing—in what I think is the least traumatic way possible. I'm very comfortable and confident."

By 1995, as a reimbursement for fundraising costs, the affiliates will get back 15 percent of all unrestricted donations that they passed along to headquarters. To get the money back, the affiliates must show that they have a plan to use the rebated money for fundraising and to develop innovative approaches to winning donations and volunteers.

The change means that the national office at first will see a drop in its own revenues. But it expects to eventually wind up with more money as divisions do a better job raising money themselves.

Employees of the Cancer Society are optimistic that the charity's shake up will work, says Robert Gadberry, who served as interim national executive vice president from 1987–1995. "It has been a long process," he says. "Those of us familiar with old ways might fear that in emphasizing process, and making so many changes, we might lose our sense of mission." However, Mr. Gadberry says, "having watched it unfold, we now have confidence we are positioning ourselves for good days ahead."

"If this fails—and I don't think it will, then we all fail together," say Mr. Poppece. "It's not something that's been imposed upon us divisions, we bought it from the very beginning." He adds: "If we can't make it work. I don't know if we would start again to put it back together."

Indeed this case reiterates our earlier discussion of the need for senior leadership to serve as sponsors for change and for patience, if not compassion, for taking the time to make thoughtful change.

Stages of Change

Field research conducted by Will Davidson, M. Oliver, P. M. Guyer, F. Almasy, and others at leading corporations over the past several years suggests that transformation occurs in interdependent phases, which can be correlated to the three stages we have identified in the nonprofit sector: reengineering, continuous improvement, and transformation (see Exhibit 9–7).

Stage 1. The transformation process begins with the redesign of service delivery and administrative processes. This first stage encompasses reengineering and utilizes automation to improve the nonprofit's service levels (quality) and productivity. (Refer to Chapter 3 for a discussion about reengineering and automation.)

Stage 2. Continuous improvement initiatives drive constituents, users, volunteers, and staff to generate effective programs and services and efficient processes. Broadly speaking, continuous quality improvement is a commitment to excellence by volunteers and staff throughout the nonprofit. Implicit in continuous quality improvement are the concepts of work groups and teams. Continuous quality improvement translates to being the best and delivering standards of service that meet or exceed the expectations of users and constituents.

Joseph Oberle, in an article entitled "Quality Gurus, the Men and Their Message" (*Training Magazine*, January 1990, pp. 47–48) summarizes the messages of the three preeminent quality gurus: W. Edwards Deming, Joseph M. Juran, and Philip B. Crosby:

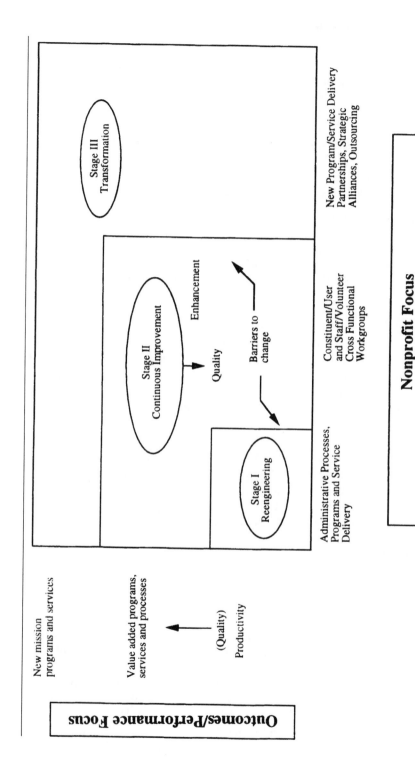

Outcomes/Performance Focus

New mission programs and services

Value added programs, services and processes

(Quality) Productivity

Stage III Transformation

New Program/Service Delivery Partnerships, Strategic Alliances, Outsourcing

Stage II Continuous Improvement

Enhancement

Quality

Barriers to change

Constituent/User and Staff/Volunteer Cross Functional Workgroups

Stage I Reengineering

Administrative Processes, Programs and Service Delivery

Nonprofit Focus

Exhibit 9-7 The Three Stages of Strategic Transformation

- Commit to quality improvement throughout your organization.
- Attack the processes, not the employees.
- Strip down the process to find and eliminate problems that diminish quality.
- Identify your customers (in our nonprofit parlance, constituents) and satisfy their requirements.
- Instill team work and create an atmosphere for innovation and permanent quality improvement.

Stage 3. Transformation can involve spin-offs, strategic alliances, and partnerships (see Chapter 7), which are new to the nonprofit sector.

There is a natural transition between each of the three stages of this model, but without astute leadership, reengineering can be stalled at Stage 1. Exhibit 9–8 summarizes some of the major differences in focus between Stage 1 reengineering and Stage 3 transformation. For example, among the objectives of reengineering are radically improved service levels and productivity. In Stage 3, the objective is the transformation or the delivery of new programs and services, within an entirely new construct or model (e.g. partnerships, and strategic alliances).

Carpe Diem: Seize the Day

In practical terms, what are the key elements to transformation? The first is vision. This vision is not of dreams, but of specific action steps to undertake your nonprofit's mission. Such vision must be grounded in, but not totally confined to, the reality of current operating conditions. Aligning current operating conditions with nonprofit vision and longer term strategies ensures that priorities are established and that there are links between short-term and long-term goals.

Although alignment of short-term and long-term initiatives is critical, often the most compelling reason for transformation is crisis. Whereas we believe it is possible to transform a nonprofit through sheer *will* rather than crisis, it is possible only with strong leadership at the staff and board levels. The case studies presented in Chapter 7 are testimony to this statement. So are the next two examples from higher education, which will forever have an impact on both the public and private sectors of higher education. The case studies have elements that are applicable to the transformation of any nonprofit organization.

Parameter	Stage 1	Stage 3
Objective	Radically improved service levels and productivity	Transformation
Time Frame	Short	Long
Leadership	Senior staff plus cross-functional work groups	Senior staff plus cross-functional work groups
Performance Focus	From a singular organization perspective: mission based, constituency driven, financial	From a multiple organization perspective: mission based, constituency driven, financial
Focus	Single and multiple processes	Nonprofit wide
Scale	Significant	Massive
Scope	Stage 1	Stages 1, 2, and 3

Exhibit 9–8 Becoming a Transformed Entity

Source: Adopted from Witt Davidson, "Beyond Reengineering: The Three Phases of Business Transformation," *IBM Systems Journal*, Vol. 32, No. 1, 1993, pp. 65–79.

CASE STUDY

Transforming the Vineyard

The history of Sonoma State University has been marked by years of tumult. Some would argue that it has been characterized by short-term and combative administrative leadership. Others would argue that the hippie values of the 1960s have found a home at Sonoma State and that these values have resulted in a campus culture characterized as permissive, lacking discipline, and contemptuous of authority.

On July 15, 1992, Dr. Reuben Arminana assumed the presidency. He described his strategy for stabilizing the institution and positioning it aggressively within the California State University System: in an interview with the author of this book in July 1994.

> Center to all my activities is the creation of a new vision of Sonoma State University. Key to the development of this vision has been our self-declaration that we are a *beta site*. A

place where taking risks is encouraged and promoted; a place where traditions are questioned and business as usual is rejected. In a sense we are trying to achieve many of the benefits of a charter campus without the political and institutional opposition that the term has elicited. A Campus Priorities Committee composed of faculty, staff and students is guiding these efforts.

Throughout his tenure, Dr. Arminana and his chief operating officer, Larry Schlereth, have worked in partnership to effect major change in the divisions of administration and finance and student affairs. These two incumbents have worked hand-in-hand with the campus vice president for academic affairs to implement a campus-wide transformation process that focuses first and foremost on the delivery of quality service to students, faculty, and staff in that priority order. The position of customer-service representative, which is charged with the responsibility of assisting students, faculty, and staff in the discharge of their administrative duties, has been created; and the classification system has been reengineered to compensate these essential staff associates at a significant level. The next step for transformation is the academic core.

Yet another transformation is occurring to the state system of higher education in Oregon. This one resulted primarily from the incredible pain experienced by each of the Oregon State System of Higher Education institutions and its chancellor's office as a result of tax reform legislation passed by the state's electorate in 1992.

CASE STUDY

Transforming a Traditional State System of Higher Education to a Public Corporation

The Higher Education Administration Efficiency Act (Senate Bill 271) of the Oregon State Legislature proposed the fundamental transformation of the entire Oregon State System of Higher Education. In 1992, Oregon State University (OSU) and Portland State University (PSU) underwent an administrative cost reduction review. This served as the first stage of administrative process reengineering not only for OSU and PSU but for the chancellor's office and the entire system itself.

Current Situation

- Significant changes have been made to reduce administrative and support costs by over $50 million over a four-year period.
- Independent consultants identified the "Oregon problem," whereby state policies require multiple layers of approvals and, therefore, increase the costs of administering the system.
- The 1993 legislature requested that the state system look at creative new ways to conduct administrative activities to further lower costs and focus resources on maintaining "a high-quality, accessible public higher education system."
- In 1995–1997, state funds will provide only 20% of the state system's $2.6 billion budget.

Proposal

- The Board of Higher Education is recommending the Administrative Efficiency Act, which, while retaining legislative oversight of the state system, will delegate administrative rules and processes to the board.
- Accountability would continue through the governor and members of the legislature, who would review the budget, student enrollment and tuition plans, special initiatives, and public services and evaluate expected outcomes from the state's investment in Oregon's public university system.
- The Board of Higher Education would establish operating policies and procedures to enable the campuses to perform administrative processes more efficiently.
- The Administrative Efficiency Act would enable the state system to operate administratively in a manner similar to Oregon's community colleges and public school districts.
- The Administrative Efficiency Act would allow the board to operate the state system in a more responsive, innovative, and entrepreneurial manner and streamline business practices so that a greater percentage of system resources

can be utilized to meet the needs of students and all Oregonians.

- Savings from increased administrative efficiencies would be utilized to teach 2,000 more Oregon undergraduate students than included in the governor's budget.

Exhibit 9–9, which was presented to the legislative committee, first summarizes the issue(s) to be addressed. The current *modus operandi* exists in the second column, and the proposed action for change appears in the third column.

Issue	Current	Proposed
1. State appropriation	Legislative appropriation	Legislative appropriation.
2. Budget authority	Legislative approval	Board will submit budget for state support to the legislative assembly for approval and will have delegated authority to budget all other funds, with annual reports to the state. Budget submitted to legislature will include a presentation of tuition and fee levels.
3. State personnel practices and collective bargaining	Dept. of Administrative Services (DAS) has authority for classified and management service employees.	OSSHE will establish its own personnel system and retain its current payroll authority. The board, rather than the DAS, will have the authority to enter into collective bargaining agreement for higher education with current unions.
4. Investment of funds	Managed by state treasurer through the Oregon Investment Council (OIC)	Managed by state treasurer though the OIC, with interest income from investments accruing to the Oregon State System of Higher Education.
5. State purchasing, contracting, and printing laws	Subject to most state provisions following DAS policies	Board will establish competitive procedures for contracting and the procurement of materials, supplies, services, and equipment, including printing.

Issue	Current	Proposed
6. Liability insurance	DAS sole provider	Board will have the option of procuring insurance coverage from DAS or may procure it elsewhere, or self-insure, if better coverage is available in an alternative manner to DAS's offered coverage.
7. Facilities and lands	Board has authority in most areas	The board will have the authority to manage and lease all property. Construction and land purchases with general fund monies will require legislative approval.
8. Social policies	Subject to state statutes and procedures governing social policies	The act will not change OSSHE's strong policies with regard to social policies. The proposed legislation asserts OSSHE's commitment to adopt policies that are designed to encourage the participation of minority-owned, women-owned, and emerging small businesses; affirmative action; recycling; the purchase of services and goods from disabled individuals; and the provision of workers' compensation to workers on contracts.

Exhibit 9–9

What does this all mean for us, the faint of heart, cautious at every turn about making waves through change? It means that we, too, can undertake change if we have the intestinal fortitude, the ability to intuit the right time to proceed with such a profound undertaking, and the will to do what we thank is right for the organization. The kind of transformation cited here and in Chapter 7 does not come easily but, oh, what can be accomplished for the greater good. Let's all seize the day with confidence.

Index